"Passion and exuberance fill this book like the sweet layers of an Appalachian stack cake. Bringing together the region's music, food, stories, and its great chefs and home cooks from among her vast circle of friends, Chef Séguret reveals the glories of Appalachian food and the rich 'soup beans, mess of greens' tradition and innovation it embodies."

—Dr. Jean Haskell, Appalachian Highlands Consulting
and co-editor of *Encyclopedia of Appalachia*

"With her classical French training and deep roots in Madison County, Susi Séguret is the perfect person to pen an ode to Appalachian cuisine. Her involvement in many regional projects and her expansive network of chefs, winemakers, farmers, and educators makes her uniquely qualified to assemble such an authoritative and colorful guide."

—Jess McCuan, Content Manager for Quid, Inc.,
Business Editor for *The San Francisco Chronicle*,
and Founding Editor of *The Asheville Scene*

"Susi Séguret's culinary education in France not only refined her talents in the kitchen, it deepened her respect for the cooking of her Madison County, North Carolina homeland. This book, filled with mountain tunes and tastes, is the loving product of that convergence. When a classically-trained chef fully understands the meaning of the measurement mountain people call a mess, you know you have something good."

—Fred Sauceman, author of the book *Buttermilk & Bible
Burgers: More Stories from the Kitchens of Appalachia*

"Every now and then, one encounters a person with great depth, energy, and resources to contribute as a volunteer to a common cause. My experience has been such with Susi in the course of years. Susi is a citizen of the world with feet resting securely on either side of the Atlantic Ocean. She continues to amaze me with her graciousness and insight along with steady work in the trenches."

—SCOTT GIVOT, CCP, CULINARY EDUCATOR, AND PRESIDENT EMERITUS OF THE INTERNATIONAL ASSOCIATION OF CULINARY PROFESSIONALS

"I have known and worked with Susi through the International Association of Culinary Professionals for years and I'm always amazed at the inventive and savvy way she approaches her business. I'd recommend her to do anything, even catering on a space shuttle. She'd figure it out."

—KATHLEEN FLINN, AWARD-WINNING AUTHOR OF *The Sharper Your Knife, the Less You Cry*, *The Kitchen Counter Cooking School*, AND *Burnt Toast Makes You Sing Good*

"There are many chefs, but few of them are also great cooks. It is a rare person to master both and to also excel at writing, photography, and making music. Susi brings together all of these and more in her life and in the writing of *Appalachian Appetite*."

—BOB BOWLES, FOUNDER OF THE ASHEVILLE WINE & FOOD FESTIVAL, SLOW FOOD ASHEVILLE, AND THE WESTERN NORTH CAROLINA WINE TRAIL

Contents

Dedication

To the chefs, farmers, producers, historians, restaurateurs, and citizens of Appalachia who contributed to this collection, and to the generations of Appalachian people who led to this moment. And, most of all, to the generations who will read this tribute and carry us forward.

Acknowledgments

WITH BOUNDLESS THANKS TO ALL WHOSE voice is expressed within these pages, and to Hatherleigh Press for picking up a flaming torch and running with it! And especially—always—to my parents, who are the reason I was born in Appalachia, and my children, who have drawn Appalachia into their hearts.

Foreword

IT IS TIME. AT LONG last, Appalachian food is emerging vibrantly from a long-time cocoon of stereotypes. With unique culinary roots deeply connected to its geography, agriculture, and traditions, it shows a creativity that ensues from the basic needs of survival combined with the independence and solidness of a mountain people surrounded with peaks and valleys.

I first encountered Susi at the 2010 Finale of the Asheville Wine & Food Festival, where we both sat on the panel of judges that awarded the prize to the most promising chef of the day—Nate Allen—who, incidentally is featured in this book. Since then, our paths have crossed many times, through activities with the International Association of Culinary Professionals and Les Dames d'Escoffier International, as well as for the 2015 opening of her Seasonal School of Culinary Arts.

I have been intrigued by Susi's passion for bringing people together over food and for singing out about the place that made her what she is. A perpetual dreamer with a solid culinary talent, she is a "connector" with the purpose of bringing her cuisine to the light.

Appalachian Appetite will indeed whet your appetite for the flavor of the mountains you can taste in the recipes found within, and for the cadence of the ballads which lead you into each chapter. Sight and sound and taste mingle on each page with the deep scents of the woods and the texture of ripe fruit which jumps out from the jar.

I am happy to share this tome with its readers, encouraging all to sip and savor its spirit of celebration, and then to lose yourselves in the kitchen and put its principles into practice!

—NATHALIE DUPREE
    James Beard Award-Winning Cookbook Author
    PBS and Food Network Host
    Grande Dame of Les Dames d'Escoffier International

"A natural adoption of local, sustainable, and organic principles means that Appalachia really should be ground zero for city-slickers planning their next culinary odyssey."
—FROM JEAN HASKELL'S *ASSESSING THE LANDSCAPE OF LOCAL FOOD IN APPALACHIA*

Preface

WHEN ASKED WHICH CUISINE MOST typifies America, chefs are bound to tell you it stems from the South. From the luscious belly of our nation, the mountains where sweet corn is grown and the rivers where the trout flashes its rainbow colors, all the way down to the Mississippi Delta, the South has a gift for capturing both our hearts and our taste buds.

If the South is the heart of America, Appalachia is the heart of the South. Our southern rivers are born high up in the Blue Ridge, our minerals are mined in West Virginia and Kentucky, our stories and songs are woven out of the Scotch-Irish culture tucked within its hills.

Huskin' bees, 'lasses boilin's, hog killin's have always been occasions to gather around a laden table where, crisped in cracklin's, the bounty of the garden is served up with generous chunks of cornbread and washed down with huge gulps of sweet tea.

Food is inevitably what holds a society together, familiar flavors linking memory to both present and past, as well as to religion and culture, creating a roadmap for generations to come.

In examining recent food trends, one might stop to ponder why Nordic cooking has gained such space with the press. It seems at first a far cry from our Appalachian hills. But its principles are our principles: making something from almost nothing, foraging the woods and the streams for whatever might be edible in times of scarcity, turning some unexpected ingredient into a feast.

"Cooking is a language through which all the following properties may be expressed: harmony, creativity, happiness, beauty, poetry, complexity, magic, humour, provocation and culture."
—FERRAN ADRIA

These same adventures in daring have made our cuisine what it is today, varied with poke sallet, wild mustard, nettles, ramps and morels, as well as squirrel, wild turkey, groundhog…we don't need the grocery store to survive.

It has been said that to understand America you must first understand Appalachia. Washington Irving, in the early 1800s, held that America should have been christened Appalachia or Alleghania instead of being confused forever by common name with the continent of South America. Edgar Allen Poe seconded his stance, preferring Appalachia as the name for a country of enterprising immigrants.

The various voices within these pages contribute to a Pan-Appalachian effort to reawaken today's American—as well as citizens from abroad—to the true essence of what Appalachia is and can be today, shaking off the dust of antiquity while valorizing the timelessness of its appeal.

Change is one of the only sureties in this precious life of ours. Change in any culture, even one which seems to move as slowly as Appalachia, is inevitable. However, some of the most wonderful elements of the Appalachia we love are the ones that even man can't alter: the blue of the mountains, the rush of water, the flash of brook trout, the glory of a misty morning, the cool of the woods, the majesty of an ancient stand of poplars.

If we look closely enough, we see that it is not Appalachia that needs changing. It is we, ourselves, who might benefit from adjusting to an Appalachian pace. How we see Appalachia is part of what shapes it. How others see Appalachia is our collective responsibility.

Introduction

AS A CHILD, I TODDLED up to the garden, intent on tasting what came from that rich black earth where my father was stirring around with his hoe. He handed me a radish, fresh from the soil, red and round, pulsing with life. I wiped off the crumbs of dirt, pulled off its beard, and took a bold bite into its crisp flesh. The unexpected and sudden burn sent me running back down the narrow path to the kitchen where my mother poured me a mug of cooling water, hauled in a bucket from the spring earlier that morning.

The spring was just downhill from a moonshine still, which I was not supposed to know about at my tender age, but I had heard my parents talking in quiet voices at night, as the crickets sang their song and lightning bugs punctuated the sky. And I had seen the clear liquid in Ball jars when neighbors came to sing ballads and play fiddle tunes into the evening. Once I picked up a jar and shook it around, and Pugin, the neighbor of the moment said, "Now honey, you set that down and don't you be foolin' with it none."

I loved the speech of these elder neighbors, loved when they brought over a package of salt pork or bacon to add to our daily diet of the Three Sisters (corn, beans, and squash), as the Cherokee called them, for their support of each other in the field.

My parents were the first outsiders to move into the hidden valley of Shelton Laurel since the turn of the 1900s when a small group of Presbyterian missionaries had come in and built a church and a school and a hospital (long since in ruins). When my parents arrived there was no paved road running through the valley. Only a dirt wagon track wound beside the small river, leading in one direction to Johnson City, Tennessee, and in the other to Greeneville, Tennessee. They had found a little loop of North Carolina, seldom crossed because of the formidable mountain roads.

If you approach by car from the flatness of Tennessee, you are unprepared for the mountains that rise up out of the blue. And they are truly blue—the Blue Ridge, or the Great Smoky Mountains, smoky because they are almost always enveloped in a haze of mist, which is humidity evaporating from their lush greenness. One moment you are looking at them in awe, and the next moment you are swallowed up by them, taken into their arms as a mother gathers a baby to her breast. And it is a similar sensation. You feel protected, nourished, suddenly a child again, and you know that all you need for life is right here, hidden in these oldest of hills.

So it was that my parents stumbled across their home-to-be after two months of camping out in farmers' fields in the surrounding area, looking for just the right spot. They had been married shortly before, and had set off in their little Volkswagen Bug with their sleeping bags and Daddy's banjo, in search of the highest mountains and the most music. (They had heard that North Carolina was a good place for the music they loved, and had looked on the map to pinpoint the mountains.) Following their nose and their ears, they ended up 50 miles north of Asheville, and lingered for a while with an old fiddler whose father offered to give them 20 acres of land if they would settle there. It was tempting, but not quite right.

Then they discovered Shelton Laurel. A secluded green valley, flanked on all sides by mountains rising gently up to 5,000 feet, it was the dream they hadn't known they had. They found an abandoned farm which they offered to rent while they searched out their own piece of land, and the 90-year-old lady who owned the farm would never take a cent from them, although they lived there two years. And she gave them fresh milk from her cow and vegetables from her garden and taught them the essentials of mountain living.

They were considered by all (locals and their northern parents alike) a little off in the head because they were educated people (Cornell and Brooklyn Museum School of Art) looking to live like the old-timers of the mountains: They wanted to build a log house, hewn on two sides in the traditional style, split shingles, raise all their food, and keep a cow, pig, chickens, and other basic farm animals. They wanted to plow with a mule (the most stubborn of all creatures, to be avoided if at all possible), carry their water, heat with a chimney, light with kerosene lamps that would need trimming every day, and (as the ultimate symbol of being behind the times) they wanted an outdoor privy.

This was in 1961, before the back-to-the-land movement began. If Peter and Polly Gott weren't pioneers in the wilderness, they were pioneers in the return to the wilderness, but they didn't have an inkling of that then. They weren't trying to prove anything. They only had a vision of how they wanted to live and set out to find it.

Not everyone was as immediately welcoming as the landlady. Strangers "never did no good." Especially "them northe'ners." In a place where nothing much happened out of the ordinary and change was so slow you didn't notice it, the Civil War was still alive in most people's memories. Even if many western Carolinians had sided with the North, figuring if they didn't have slaves, "by God, nobody else oughtta have 'em either." And they didn't need "nobody from the outside comin' in and tellin' 'em what to do, neither."

Lucky for Daddy, he brought his 5-string along. Everybody, even the most taciturn, loved music. And they'd all ask him, "atter-a-while," "if'n he could play that thang." Just a verse of "Old Joe Clark" would bring smiles to faces, and some of the neighbors would kick up their heels and do a step or two. And some would say, "Here, give me that banjer, son, and let me show ye how my grandaddy done it." There were those, like old man Uncle George Landers, who hadn't touched an instrument in years and who'd get all excited and remember tune after tune. At night, after the chores were done, Daddy would try to remember what he heard, and the next time he saw a neighbor he could play it back note for note.

Soon he was calling square dances in another rented shack, and finding local people to play for them. Nobody had thought about calling dances in years because there was always so much trouble afterward. Shelton Laurel was in a dry county, so there was a lot of illegal whiskey made by the light of the moon. That, combined with Scotch-Irish tempers, was a volatile invitation to "have it out." But young Pete was just naïve (or ignorant, whichever way you want to put it) enough so that he didn't think twice about giving the dances another try. And people came. "Swing your partner, do-si-do, promenade 'round with a heel 'n toe. Boy, that young man c'n pick a banjer, and he c'n call them squar' dances too!"

Later, after we had moved into the log house of my parents' building, on 40 acres of steep wooded land which they bought for $40 an acre, the word began to circulate up north about a homesteading couple who were doing everything by hand, and living on $200 a year: $3 for the kerosene to fill their oil lamps, $10 for seeds to plant their garden, $8 for coffee, and $8 for toilet paper (they had

tried corn shucks and newspapers and even mullein leaves for a commended amount of time, and had given in to that one luxury), with what was left over for local taxes and a little gasoline.

So we started having visitors. Of course we had no telephone to warn us of their arrival, and they would just appear. And stay. The back-to-the-land movement had begun, and young hippie couples were looking for role models. I don't know how the word got around so well, but I remember people spread out in sleeping bags all over our living room floor, and sometimes even lining the floor of our henhouse. And my mother spending long hours over the hot stove when I knew she wanted to be out painting. Or working with her clay (she had made the middle story of our cow barn into a functioning potter's studio). It was lucky Mother and Daddy had planted a big garden. And dug a deep outhouse.

So, by and large, the young couple was adopted, and there were many who came to help them out and show them things about canning, basket-making, harvesting, tanning ground-hog hides. And there were those, too, who drove up and stood by, their hands in their pockets whistling, looking on to see how "them crazy young'uns was a-makin' it."

When, almost 30 years later, I moved from the sorghum fields of Appalachia to the wheat fields of France, following the musical muse, I encountered a similar welcome as a stranger to a small village where nothing much had changed for centuries. There were new tastes to assimilate along with several hundred cheeses to meet firsthand (hello 20 pounds, goodbye waist!), not to mention an arsenal of wines.

With two decades of spreading Appalachian music and tastes around Europe under my belt, I yielded to the constant lure of North Carolina, trading croissants back in for cornbread. Once again I gathered ramps and chestnuts, kept chickens and dealt with the ensuing possums (who like to frequent chicken houses) by putting them in the pot with shallots and Dijon mustard and white wine, a touch of France plus Appalachia, or "Frappalachia," as I have come to call it.

The pages that follow represent a blending together of old ingredients and new techniques, of the standard flavors that everyone loves about Appalachia and that extra twist, when appropriate, to lead those around the table into ecstasy.

There is a mixture of the basic and the sublime, the celebrated chef's favorite and the home cook's standby. From Mississippi to Maine (where the Appalachian Trail comes to a halt on top of Mount Katahdin), innovation and reverence for what is close at hand is the continuum for both cook and connoisseur. So grab a skillet, and dive into an Appalachian Appetite!

"With today's emphasis on organically-grown, humanely-raised food that travels only a short distance from the farm to the table, chefs are rediscovering the timeless wisdom of the Appalachian worldview."
—FRED SAUCEMAN

Appalachian
Elements

Defining the Appalachian Region

The Appalachian Region, as defined by the Appalachian Regional Commission, is a 205,000-square-mile region that follows the spine of the Appalachian Mountains from southern New York to northeastern Mississippi. It includes all of West Virginia and parts of 12 other states: Alabama, Georgia, Kentucky, Maryland, Mississippi, New York, North Carolina, Ohio, Pennsylvania, South Carolina, Tennessee, and Virginia. Forty-two percent of the Region's population is rural, compared with 20 percent of the national population.

The ARC-defined region (based on politics and economics) includes 420 counties in 13 states. It extends more than 1,000 miles and is home to more than 25 million people.

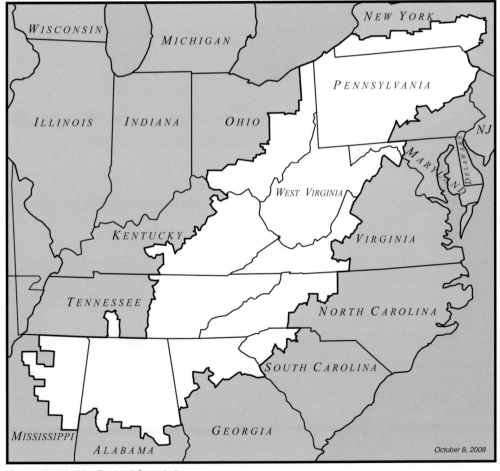

October 8, 2008

Source: Appalachian Regional Commission

A more geographic definition has Appalachia reaching all the way up through the New England states and into Maine, where the Appalachian Trail reaches its final point at the top of Mount Katahdin. The Appalachian Mountains, as defined by the US Geological Survey, span across five geologic provinces: the Appalachian Basin, the Blue Ridge Mountains, the Piedmont Province, the Adirondack Province (although the Adirondacks are actually part of the Laurentian Shield), and the New England Province. This definition brings at least six more states into the picture: Connecticut, New Jersey, Massachusetts, Vermont, New Hampshire and Maine. Technically, the foundation of the Appalachian Mountains reaches up as far as Quebec and Newfoundland.

Whatever the physical definition, the essence of Appalachia is its heart, which beats within each of its inhabitants past and present, reaching back in time to the Cherokee and Pisgah peoples who once roamed its forests, embracing the European settlers who courageously made it their home, and welcoming those who now seek solace into the folds of its lush, blue mountains, where nourishment is always to be found.

*"Appalachia boasts one of the—if not **the**—strongest, most original, and most consistent regional cuisines in America."*
—FROM JEAN HASKELL'S
 ASSESSING THE LANDSCAPE OF LOCAL FOOD IN APPALACHIA

Appalachian Style or Southern Style?

Within the broader umbrella of Southern cooking lie the recipes that are indigenous to Appalachia but not necessarily to the rest of the South. How might one define Appalachian style as separate from Southern style?

Part of that distinction has a geological explanation, as the Appalachian region is defined by its mountains, and as such, certain species, both animal and plant which may be found readily in the larger scope of the South are not found in the mountains. Likewise, many species are found only in Appalachia and not in the low country, or in the remainder of the country, for that matter.

Author Ashley English writes, "What differentiates Appalachian cooking from Southern cuisine can be largely distilled down to ingredients. The mountains made travel difficult and cumbersome, so food production and preparation for this region's ancestors all took place close to home. Furthermore, factor in a lack of electricity, and it became even more imperative that foods needed to be grown and preserved here, both easily and expediently. Pigs, chickens, corn, beans, pumpkin, wild greens, wild nuts, wild mushrooms, and fields of cane rendered into sorghum grew well here, and came to define the southern Appalachian culinary repertoire. Anything that didn't grow here was largely absent from kitchen tables, going on to define the sub-genres of other areas of the southern U.S."

Another distinction between Appalachia and the South at large is one of financial wealth. While much of the educated South was privy to old family money, almost none of Appalachia had the resources to augment their meager crops with any extravagance. Appalachian culture developed largely out of poverty while Southern culture developed largely out of wealth. Thus, as historian Dr. Katie Hoffman points out, Appalachian cooking tends to rely on meat more as a flavoring and less as a main dish, eked out by vegetables, some of which, like the sweet potato, could stand in for sugar as well.

Technically, Appalachia is as northern as it is southern, with as much of the mountainous chain stretching in each direction from the Mason-Dixon line. So what sets Appalachian people apart is more a quality of mountain wisdom than one of a frozen position in the Civil War. In fact, in Madison County, North Carolina (my home of birth and of the heart), more citizens fought for the North than for the South. They are a proud people, influenced far less than the rest of the country by political affiliations. They have needed to be tough to

survive their geographical isolation, and if they seemed to scorn outside help it is only because they knew the value of self-reliance.

Of the areas that lie both in the South and in Appalachia, one might say that they are blessed with the best of both worlds. Their people embody simultaneously the legendary hospitality of the South and the resourcefulness and perseverance of the mountain folk. Their culinary contributions are, if not as lavish as unguarded resources might allow, at least as luscious as the forests and streams and the richness of imagination that have fed them.

Jeff Biggers writes, in *The United States of Appalachia: How Southern Mountaineers Brought Independence, Culture, and Enlightenment to America*, "few regions in the United States confound and fascinate Americans like Appalachia." In recent times, best-selling authors Barbara Kingsolver, Charles Frazier, Homer Hickam, Lee Smith, and Robert Morgan have spun their tales in and around Appalachia. The James Beard House has hosted numerous dinners featuring Appalachian chefs (William Dissen, Nate Allen, and Richard and Anne Arbaugh) and other Appalachian chefs have recently been awarded the accolade of JBA outstanding chef (Sean Brock, Kevin Gillespie, Edward Lee, Steven Satterfield, and Tandy Wilson).

All up and down the Appalachian chain, chefs and growers and restaurateurs are transforming our collective belief system by showing us that life *can* still be lived simply, that eating is not only an act of necessity; it is an act of joy.

"Appalachian food is the backbone of the South."
—Alison Sher, *Best Chefs America*

Music & Food:
The Double Essence of Appalachia

Food and music in Appalachia have always been intertwined, as illustrated in the titles of a multitude of fiddle tunes and ballads: "Bile 'em Cabbage Down," "Groundhog," "Old Joe Clark," "Mountain Dew," "Cornbread, Molasses & Sassafras Tea," "Shortenin' Bread," "Walkin' in My Sleep," "Leather Britches," "The Crawdad Song," and endless others.

Music and food are two elements we will always need for survival, whether we live in Appalachia or in any other part of the globe. Food feeds our body while music feeds our soul. The concept of Note-by-Note Cooking, developed by French father of molecular gastronomy, Hervé This, equates separate molecules of flavor with individual notes of the musical scale. In combination they form a chord, and when the right chords unite, you end up with a symphony to the senses. "In the hands of a great cook," says This, "a meal is capable of touching us as a love song does."

Pig pickin's and ramp festivals, turkey shoots, 'lasses boilin's, must all have their musical component to be complete, be it in the form of a hired band or an impromptu breaking into ballad singing as the appearance of stars announces the cool of evening.

In 1916, Cecil Sharp, an English ballad collector, happened into the hills of Appalachia, in search of songs long forgotten in the Old Country. He found, in Madison County, North Carolina, the ballads he was seeking, passed down from one generation to another, often dozens of verses long—verses of love and

longing, of daring adventure, of courtship and hardship, of tilling the land, rocking babies, burying loved ones.

Many were playful, often nonsensical. Others were eerily haunting, a link between men and women and their Maker. Verses that have endured through journeys across oceans, trips across mountains, in generations of working men and women, ring out to this day over the holler:

Old Joe Clark had a great big house
Sixteen stories high
And every story in that house
Was filled with chicken pie...

Or Bascom Lamar Lunsford's time-honored recipe of the favorite beverage of many:

Well, you take a little trash
And you mix it with ash
And the soul of an old worn-out shoe
Well, you stir it a while
With an old rusty file
And you call it that good old mountain dew...

And the enchanting:

Well, come along girls and listen to my noise
Don't you marry them Arkansas boys
Marry you a guy from Tennessee
And eat cornbread, molasses and sassafras tea,
Cornbread, molasses and sassafras tea...

Notes penetrate the hills and drift out across the corn fields when the day's work is done. Music is as natural as breathing, passed on almost by osmosis— as good cooking is when generations abide under one roof. Fiddles sing, banjos ring, toes tap, old folks clap, and the youth look on taking it all in with wide eyes, tradition seeping in as it has for generations before and will continue to do in generations to come.

Appalachian Ingredients

A good recipe begins with good ingredients. A great recipe allows the touch of the master's hand (the cook, the chef) to enhance these ingredients so that they are planted indelibly in your, the eater's, memory. The unequalled richness of Appalachia's floral and faunal resources allows a playfulness which the world beyond is only beginning to discover. Below are a few of Appalachia's treasures.

Acorns
Bear
Black walnuts
Branch lettuce
Chanterelles
Chestnuts
Collards
Coon
Corn
Creasy greens
Dandelions
Deer
Ginseng
Greenbriar shoots

Groundhog
Grouse
Hickory nuts
Leather britches
May apples
Moonshine
Morels
Mustard greens
Okra
Pawpaws
Pokeweed
Persimmons
Rabbit
Ramps

Sassafras
Sourwood honey
Spicebush
Squirrel
Stinging nettles
Sumac
Sweet birch
Trout
Turkey foot
Venison
Violets
Wild boar
Wild ginger
Wild turkey

"The most precious ingredient in Appalachian cookery is time. Time to plant and nurture seeds of corn and beans. Time to cultivate fields of cane through spring, summer, and fall, and boil down the juice over a hot fire in October to produce the precious thick sweetness of sorghum syrup. Time to cure a pig and wait more than a year for the reward of country ham. Time to learn from a grandmother and perpetuate her traditions."

—FRED SAUCEMAN

The Recipes

A Note on Timing

By a twist of fate, the bulk of this manuscript was compiled in the springtime, with the main ingredient of my surrounding woods being ramps, seconded by morels. Hence, the abundance of recipes containing these two ingredients. If I had been compiling the recipes in the summertime, tomatoes, peppers, and sweet corn would surely have dominated. By the same token, had the moment fallen in autumn or early winter, apples, pumpkins, and chestnuts would have been featured.

Ideally, the period of writing would encompass several seasons, and would permit extensive travel all up and down the Appalachian chain to test and re-test recipes, and to gather them personally from targeted chefs. Since timing is of necessity a factor, the selection of recipes to follow—and the selection of chefs who contributed them—is a modest slice of a larger picture, a hearty appetizer which I hope will inspire you, the reader, to meander widely through Appalachia, tasting your way through endless expressions of this endearing region.

A Note on Pepper and Salt

For all recipes, unless otherwise noted, use freshly ground black pepper (pre-ground pepper does not compare for a minute!) and sea salt. Salt needs vary according to purpose, but the majority of the recipes will taste best if a large-grained sea salt such as La Baleine or Diamond Crystal are used. I personally do not care for the consistency of kosher salt, but many chefs consider it a standby. If you want fine salt, unless a large quantity is called for, try grinding fresh large-grained salt onto your dish. If you have access to salt from J.Q. Dickinson Salt-Works in West Virginia, you will be seasoning your dishes with the salt of Appalachia itself!

A Note on Measurements

Quantities are something to be adjusted to the taste of each chef and to how many are being served at any given meal. I have made a valiant effort to cite quantities for the sake of those who require a precise estimate, but many of these are, at best, only approximate.

Recipes are living, growing entities. They come alive under the hands of some and seem to stagnate under the hands of others. Two people can take the very same recipe, quantities or no quantities, and the dish will come out differently depending on the mood of the person, the temperature of the day, the hurriedness or leisureliness with which the dish is prepared, the quality of the ingredients, the preciseness of the measurer, the speed of the hand with which the sauce is stirred…

One thing is certain: You have only failed if you haven't tried. Dare. Plunge in. Guess. Have fun. And remember, some things are not meant to be set in stone.

A Note on Beverage Pairing

While nothing beats fresh mountain spring water or sweet tea to accompany a true Appalachian meal, and while children will often opt for fresh cow's milk or buttermilk, the alcoholic spirits of Appalachia are varied and plentiful. In addition to a multitude of moonshine sources, both legal and dubious, the region has become home to a dizzying array of micro-breweries (Asheville was voted Beer City USA no less than four times in a row), and has been springing up wineries at an impressive rate, making up for the lost years of prohibition. North Carolina alone has well over 100 wineries and three AVAs (recognized American Viticultural Areas) at the time of writing. In addition, ciderworks are multiplying as old orchards are being brought back to life and new orchards planted.

Always an advocate of sourcing beverages from the area in which the food was gathered, I encourage you, the reader, to try as many of the local beverages as you possibly can, particularly the wines, which are rapidly gaining in reputation. With truffles, wine, and the finest of vegetables, meats and dairy products at our fingertips, there is no longer any reason to think of Appalachia as a poverty-struck, under-advantaged region. I predict that, in the years beginning now, the whole world will be looking our way, as it wakes up to the reality that simple is wonderful, and the future can be brilliantly sprouted from tradition, when that tradition is revered and heard.

"Our recipes tell us everything about us: where we live, what we value, how we spend our time..."
—LEE SMITH

A Savory Start

Tidbits to slip you into a mountain trance

One of mountain music's most popular fiddle tunes, recorded by hundreds of artists and played by millions, Texas fiddler Eck Robertson's release of "Sally Goodin" was the number one country music bestseller for the year 1923.

Sally Goodin

(Traditional)

Little piece of pie, little piece of
    puddin'
Give it all away just to see Sally
    Goodin

Had a piece of pie an' I had a piece of
    puddin'
An' I give it all away just to see my
    Sally Goodin

Love a 'tater pie an' I love an apple
    puddin'
An' I love a little gal that they call
    Sally Goodin

Dropped the 'tater pie an' I left the
    apple puddin'
I went across the mountain for to see
    my Sally Goodin

Well, I looked down the road an' I see
    my Sally comin'
An' I thought to my soul that I'd kill
    myself a-runnin'

I'm goin' up the mountain an' marry
    little Sally
Raise corn on the hillside an' the
    devil in the valley

Rainin' an' a-pourin' an' the creek's
    runnin' muddy
An' I'm so in love that I can't stand
    steady

Raspberry pie, huckleberry puddin',
Give it all away for to see Sally
    Goodin.

Denny's Pickled Ramps

Denny Trantham

Denny Trantham is the ultimate southern gentleman, a towering yet soft-spoken bear of a man, he airs his Dutch Cove roots to all who dare taste his smashed potatoes laced with butter and his turnip greens, tendered up with his ever-present secret ingredient: bacon fat. Long-time Executive Chef of Asheville's iconic Grove Park Inn, Denny had the honor of feeding President and Michelle Obama for four days on the occasion of their first visit to Asheville. He and his crew slept in the kitchen and worked around the clock. The ultimate compliment was the moment when the First Lady reached out and started eating smashed potatoes right out of the serving dish. "At the end of the day," as Chef Trantham is fond of saying, "that's when you know you've made people happy." Denny's take on pickled ramps brings in a little bit of heat from the Orient for an unexpected additional kick. If you are unable to find ramps, try the same with spring onions, adding a few garlic cloves for character, keeping in mind that the effect will be much subtler. And if you have no Oriental spices at hand, by all means substitute whatever hot peppers may have grown in your garden.

1 pound ramps bulbs (or whole ramps), trimmed and washed
1 cup granulated sugar
1 cup rice wine vinegar
1 cup water
1 tablespoon kosher salt (or ½ tablespoon table salt)
1 tablespoon Japanese seven spice (Shichimi Togarashi)
1½ teaspoons Korean crushed red pepper (Kochukaru) or other mild crushed chili pepper

Bring a saucepan of water to boil. Briefly blanch the ramp bulbs in salted water. If using entire young ramp (small bulb and leaves) there is no need to blanch. Drain and set aside.

Combine all ingredients except the ramp bulbs in the saucepan over medium-high heat. Bring to a boil, whisking until the sugar has dissolved. Turn off the heat and add the ramp bulbs to the brine mixture in the pan. Let cool to room temperature and then transfer to a smaller non-reactive container, cover tightly, and place in the refrigerator overnight. You could also can the pickled ramp bulbs. *For a note about sustainable ramp harvesting, see page 205.*

Mark's Pickled Ramps

Mark Rosenstein

Mark Rosenstein opened the first farm-to-table fine dining restaurant in Asheville in the '70s, before farm-to-table had become a byword, and before French was chic in a tobacco-trading town. Over the years his innovation has inspired countless chefs to think beyond the ordinary and to let the ingredients shine for what they are. For those who wish to take ramp—or any—pickling to another level, here are some variables you might consider.

About Pickling Equipment

When you pickle, there is a high level of acidity. For this reason use stoneware, pottery, glass, or stainless steel equipment only. Do not use aluminum or iron cookware. Use either stainless steel or wooden spoons. All pickles should be packed in sterile jars.

About Water Bath Processing

The boiling water bath process is used for acid fruits and brined vegetables. You can use a pressure canner with a bottom rack for this purpose. To process, fill the canner to about jar height with water, and bring it to a boil. When the water is boiling, lower the sealed jars into the water bath. Add additional boiling water if necessary to cover the jars by one inch. Process for 30 minutes. Add water as necessary. Add one minute of processing time for every 1,000 feet in altitude. Do not let the jars touch while they are processing. Remove the jars with tongs once the processing is finished, and allow to cool in a draft-free place.

Several generous bunches of fresh ramps, cleaned

For the Salt Soak

1 tablespoon salt per quart of water

10% brine solution (1½ cups salt per gallon of water), to cover

White vinegar (5%–6% acidity level)

Sugar (mixed in proportion of 1 cup sugar to 1 gallon vinegar)

Per jar

½-inch-long red hot pepper pod

6 whole coriander seeds

Small bay leaf

Small piece of mace

3 cloves without the head

Mix together water and salt in the proportion of 1 tablespoon per quart of water. Soak the cleaned ramps in this solution for 2 hours. Drain. Then soak the ramps in a 10% brine solution for 48 hours. Drain. Bring sugar and vinegar just to a boil, in the proportion of 1 cup of sugar to 1 gallon of vinegar. Add the ramps, and simmer for 2 minutes. Pack in sterile quart canning jars. Add to each jar the red pepper, coriander, bay leaf, mace, and cloves without heads. Cover with the vinegar. Process for 30 minutes in a boiling water bath. Allow to cool.

Grits (or Polenta) with Morels

Serves 6

Mark Rosenstein

3 cups cooked grits or polenta
1 cup dried morels, rehydrated,
    drained, liquid reserved (or
    fresh morels, if you are lucky
    enough to have them!)
2 shallots
1 apple, peeled, cored, diced
2 tablespoons cooking oil
½ teaspoon cumin, ground
½ teaspoon caraway, ground
1 tablespoon apple cider vinegar
3 tablespoons apple cider
1 tablespoon reduced chicken
    stock
Reserved rehydration liquid
    from morels
Mascarpone (optional)
Salt and pepper to taste

Make grits or polenta according to directions, and keep warm. Peel and dice the shallot. Peel, core and dice the apple. In a non-aluminum saucepan, over medium heat, sauté the shallot and apple until soft. Season with salt, pepper and the ground spices. Add the cider vinegar and allow to evaporate. Add the apple cider, the reduced chicken stock and the reserved liquid from the morels. Simmer 1 minute then add the rehydrated morels. Cook for 3 minutes. Portion the grits or polenta onto warm plates and spoon the morels over the top. Garnish if you wish with a dollop of mascarpone.

Cast Iron Fried Scrapple Croquette
with Fresh Poached Quail Egg, Green Tomato and Rhubarb Chow Chow, and Smoky Hollandaise Soup on Roasted Corn and Bacon Hash

Anne Hart

Anne Hart operates Provence Market Café in Bridgeport, West Virginia. Provence Market Café's menu offers South of France-inspired, community-supported cuisine. This dish was given a perfect score in the 2003 Cast Iron Cook-Off where Anne and her team not only paired their West Virginia-sourced ingredients with West Virginia wines; they appeared in handsome chef coats made of Dorothy Draper fabric, matching the interior design of the Greenbriar Resort where the competition was held. This is a tribute to the earthiness of West Virginia with the refinement worthy of the best French chef. (Have heart—or Hart, if you will!— The rest of the recipes, with the exception of one or two, are much simpler! This is to start you off with a bang.)

For the Scrapple

1 pound ground Gardner Farm's (or your local butcher's) pork

2 cups bacon stock (2 cups water with 1 tablespoon + 1 teaspoon bacon base)

¾ teaspoon ground sage

1 cup Ground Bloody Butcher (or your closest local) corn meal, ground fine

½ teaspoon mixed salt and pepper

Fine corn meal for dusting scrapple

Oil for frying

A few fresh sage leaves

Dash of smoked paprika

Bring water to simmer in stockpot. Add pork, bacon base, and seasonings. Break up pork with a slotted spatula into fine pieces until it is no longer pink. Add corn meal. Continue to cook over medium heat until thick, about 10 minutes.

Spray a shallow half sheet pan with oil and line with plastic wrap. Spread the pork mixture evenly. Fold plastic wrap over top and weigh down with another deep half sheet pan filled with ice. Place pans in an iced foam cooler.

Portion scrapple into twelve 1½ tablespoon-size balls and roll in fine corn meal. Place balls back in cooler until ready for use. Fry in hot vegetable oil to cover, until browned, and remove to paper towels. Slightly flatten the balls.

For the Corn and Bacon Hash

1 cup fresh frozen shucked corn
4 ounces small-diced bacon
2 tablespoons diced scallions
Salt and pepper to taste

Fry diced smoked bacon until almost crisp. Remove to a small stainless bowl. Add corn to sauté pan and sauté until slightly browned. Add diced scallions. Salt and pepper to taste. Remove to a separate stainless bowl. At service, combine the corn and bacon mixture to heat.

For the Smoky Hollandaise Soup

4 tablespoons butter
4 cups chicken stock (4 cups water to 1 tablespoon chicken base)
2 tablespoons corn starch in slurry (additional 2 tablespoons corn starch in slurry backup)
3 egg yolks
¼ cup heavy cream
2 tablespoons lemon juice
½ teaspoon chipotle powder
Salt and pepper to taste

Bring water to boil. Melt butter in a saucepan. Add chicken base and butter to boiling water. Bring to a boil and add the first slurry. Continue to boil a couple of minutes. Add lemon juice. In a separate bowl, beat the egg yolks. Add the cream to the egg yolks and incorporate. Right before service, temper the eggs with the hot liquid. Add the egg mixture to the stock. Add the chipotle to a bit of the reserved slurry to break up clumps. Check for desired thickness. Add the additional slurry if necessary. Portion with a 3-ounce ladle into small pitchers.

For the Green Tomato and Rhubarb Chow Chow

1 cup sugar
½ cup apple cider vinegar
1 teaspoon minced garlic
½ cup diced yellow onions
½ cup golden raisins
½ cup diced rhubarb
2 cups diced green tomato
(1 large)
1 small finely minced cayenne
pepper
Salt and pepper to taste

Combine sugar and vinegar in a skillet and heat over medium flame. Meanwhile, chop all ingredients and add (with the exception of the garlic) to skillet. Cook over medium heat for ½ hour, adding the garlic during the last 10 minutes. Remove to cool when mixture thickens.

For the Poached Quail Eggs

12 quail eggs (if unable to locate quail eggs, see if you can find some fresh pullet eggs, which are smaller in size)
½ cup champagne vinegar
Ice, enough to cool eggs

Bring 6 inches of water to simmer in a stockpot. Add champagne vinegar to water. Tap top of quail egg with heavy knife. Using a small sharp knife cut away the top of the egg. Fill small ramekins with 1 teaspoon Champagne vinegar. Gently pour each opened quail egg into a separate ramekin, on top of the vinegar. Let sit.

Making a vortex in the water, gently drop each egg into the simmering water, three at a time. Remove after exactly 60 seconds with a slotted spoon and place directly into an ice bath. At service, drop each egg back into the simmering water to heat, about 10 seconds. Remove to paper towels to drain, cutting off tail, if any. Plate immediately, starting with a small ladleful of the hollandaise soup, in the center of which you place a spoonful of the hash, on which you will place the scrapple topped with the quail egg and garnished with fresh sage.

Tennessee Corn & Truffle Flan

Tom Michaels & Vicki Blizzard

A version of this beguiling recipe, from Vicki's family—with Tom's addition of his Tennessee Truffles*—was included in Molly O'Neill's 2007 New York Times article "Coveted, French, and Now in Tennessee", which impacted my life in more ways than I can begin to explain here (that is another story!). Also featured in Vicki's Jessiehouse, Georgia family cookbook, as well as The Blackberry Farm Cookbook, it is a fine example of how the mundane can be made sublime by the addition of one special (and I do mean exceptionally special!) ingredient.

¼ cup flour

½ cup fine cornmeal

1 tablespoon sugar

¼ teaspoon baking soda

⅛ teaspoon sea salt

2 cups fresh or frozen corn kernels

½ cup unsalted butter, melted

2 large eggs, beaten well

Dash of cayenne pepper

2 cups sour cream

1 cup grated Parmesan cheese

1 to 2 ounces finely shaved fresh black winter truffle (*Tuber melanosporum*)

Preheat oven to 325°F. In a bowl, combine flour, cornmeal, sugar, baking soda, and sea salt. Set aside. If using frozen corn, make sure it is well-defrosted and drained.

In a nonstick skillet over high heat, toss corn until slightly dry and toasted. In a bowl, combine cooked corn with 7 tablespoons melted butter, the eggs, cayenne, and sour cream. Using a few swift strokes, add dry ingredients. Stir in cheese and shaved truffle, reserving just enough truffle to garnish flan before serving.

Use remaining tablespoon butter to grease eight 6-ounce ramekins. Spoon mixture into ramekins, cover each with foil and place in a baking pan. Add boiling water to pan until it reaches halfway up ramekins. Bake for 25 minutes. Remove from oven and allow to rest, covered, for 10 minutes before serving. Flan can be served in ramekins, garnished with additional truffle slices, or loosened and turned out on a plate.

Author's Note: The black winter truffle (Tuber melanosporum), also known as the Perigord Truffle, is not an ingredient one would usually expect to find included in an Appalachian cookbook. The fruity, musky, floral, earthy fungus is usually associated with Italy or with the south of France, where dogs and sometimes pigs root them out from under their host oak and hazelnut trees. However, the  *limestone hills of East Tennessee may be coaxed into growing this elusive and cherished ingredient, as can the tobacco fields of North Carolina and Virginia, and even West Virginia. Champion of this venture, following Franklin Garland's first successful harvest of a specimen in Hillsborough, North Carolina, in 1992, is Dr. Tom Michaels of Tennessee Truffle. The thought that the historically poorest region in America can produce the most coveted and costly culinary ingredient in the world is reason for all to celebrate!*

"To tell the story of the truffle is to tell the history of world civilization."
—ALEXANDRE DUMAS

Maine Diver Scallops with Corn Nage

James Boyce

Alabama chef and multiple restaurant owner James Boyce lives by the motto "Eat Simply. Eat Smart. Eat Well." Sound advice. Nager in French means to swim; thus, this dish is essentially a corn base in which the scallops are swimming.

1 shallot, sliced thinly
2 tablespoons whole butter
1 cup fresh Silver Queen*,
   or other white corn
2 cups chicken stock
¼ cup heavy cream
1 teaspoon olive oil
12 Maine diver scallops,
   patted dry
Salt and pepper to taste

*Silver Queen is a variety of corn which yields a small harvest. The Amish grow it in the Tennessee Valley. It is a mixed ear with both white and yellow kernels. The taste is similar to other local favorites.

Place shallot and butter in a heavy saucepan and sweat slightly. Add corn to pan with chicken stock and heavy cream, and cook for 7 minutes. Allow to cool slightly and purée in a food processor until smooth, using care as with any hot liquid. Adjust seasoning to taste and hold warm.

Meanwhile, place a large skillet on medium-high heat and allow oil to heat. When oil is very hot, but not smoking, place seasoned scallops in pan. Cook on each side for two minutes, allowing a golden crust to form. Remove from pan and keep warm.

Presentation
Spoon the corn nage onto a warm tray and place scallops on top, or spoon on individual plates and place a scallop in the center of each.

Baked Sweet Potato Canapés
with Pistachio Mint Pesto and Goat Cheese

Debby Maugans

When Debby Maugans—long-time food writer for The Birmingham News—moved to Asheville, the cultural richness of the Appalachian mountains gave her a new sense of purpose. Below is her fresh take on what to do with sweet potatoes.

1 pound sweet potatoes, peeled and cut into ⅛-inch thick slices
2 tablespoons extra virgin olive oil
Pistachio Parsley Mint Pesto
Goat cheese (about 3 ounces)
Salt and pepper to taste

Preheat oven to 400°F. Place potato slices, in an even layer, on a rimmed baking sheet covered with a piece of parchment paper. Brush both sides of potatoes with olive oil and sprinkle lightly with salt and pepper.

Roast until browned on bottom, 10 to 15 minutes; flip and roast until tender and lightly browned on the other side, about 10 minutes. Transfer to a platter.

On each slice, spoon a dollop of goat cheese and pesto.

For the Pistachio Parsley Mint Pesto
Makes ½ cup
2 tablespoons minced fresh flat-leaf parsley
2 tablespoons minced fresh mint
2 tablespoons finely chopped roasted shelled pistachios
1 tablespoon freshly grated Parmesan cheese
1 tablespoon extra virgin olive oil
¼ teaspoon grated lemon rind
1 small clove garlic, minced
Salt and pepper to taste

Place first seven ingredients in a small bowl and mix well. Season to taste with salt and pepper.

Trout Marrow

Nate Allen

Nate Allen is one of the most charismatic and innovative chefs I have run across in my years since entering the awe-inspiring realm of the chef's world. Numerous times he has conducted a class for my summer session of the Seasonal School of Culinary Arts, and he keeps us all in suspense, as he never announces what he might prepare or what ingredients he might need, let alone provide quantities of anything for commemoration. He cooks by instinct, as is my personal preference, but that does not facilitate the task of capturing any of his magic for duplication.

The below recipe is the only one I have ever known him to set down, and apart from the 20 specified rainbow trout (I hope you have a lot of guests!), your guess is probably as good as his, as to the quantities of ingredients. This is what keeps cooking alive, what creates the surprises we all love. At any given time a recipe will turn out differently because of the guess factor, even in the hands of the same chef.

Nate regards this recipe as one of his greatest personal achievements, and shares it with slight reluctance. If you can bring about an ounce of his magic and his pleasure in creating this phenomenon, then you will have succeeded in a grand rite of passage!

20 large rainbow trout

Large-grain salt for 5% brine

Sugar for 5% brine

Pinch of pepper

2 bay leaves

2 sprigs thyme

2 peppercorns

1 tablespoon olive oil

Juice of 1 lemon

White wine for fumet and to top off quart jars

Heavy cream to top off quart jars

½ teaspoon agar agar

First, filet and decapitate 20 large rainbow trout. Remove the tail fin from each trout spine using meat shears, and use fin along with rib bones to make fumet.

Brine the heads and spines and all their remaining attached meat in a 5% salt and 5% sugar brine for 24 hours. Remove from the brine and arrange spines on a full sheet tray. They should all fit without overlapping. Arrange the heads facing upward, using the collars for support on a separate half sheet or hotel pan. Set your oven to 190°F. The bodies will need to roast at this low temperature for approximately five minutes, just until the meat starts to slip from the bone but remains translucent like the color and texture of cold smoked salmon. If your oven is uneven or non-convection, then you should rotate the sheet after two minutes. The heads need to cook for 10 to 15 minutes or until the lower jaw bone easily releases from the skull to expose the perfect cheek meat.

Pick the meat as quickly as possible from the bones, and spread out on parchment, on a new full sheet tray, to ensure its continual cooling. As soon as you harvest all your meat you can toss it with a pinch of pepper, 1 tablespoon of olive oil, and the juice of one medium-sized lemon. Then pack tightly into a pan or a jar, press plastic wrap onto its exposed surface area, and put it in the fridge to set up for two hours. This is an amazing trout terrine that allows for total meat usage with no waste.

But wait…there's more! Now that you have a pile of skulls and cleaned trout spines, put the heads into your fumet pot with the fins and ribs, and remember never to let this boil, but brew it like tea and let it sit in hot water with aromatics and wine for up to an hour before straining. This produces absolute clarity, which we will need to complete this ludicrous recipe.

Place all spines into two quart mason jars. Break them in half if you need to; remain in total control of the wily bones. Fill the jars with equal parts white wine, heavy cream, and trout fumet. Add a sprig of thyme and one lightly charred fresh bay laurel leaf to each jar, along with one peppercorn. Seal with new rings and lids, and pressure can for 45 minutes at 15 psi. Make sure that you have enough water in the pressure canner and that you keep your pressure steady. It is easy to break jars with this routine.

Once you carefully remove the jars and allow them to cool you can transfer the contents of one jar to a robot coupe and add ¼ teaspoon agar agar and purée until relatively smooth. Pass this purée into a sauce pan through a chinois mousseline (fabric), and reserve the bones. Repeat this process with the other jar. Bring your liquid to a boil, then transfer to a container to cool and store. This usually sets up in about an hour and is your first texture of the marrow.

Then take the remaining bone matter and place it in a spice grinder and grind like there's no tomorrow! Once you have achieved crunchy peanut butter consistency you have your second texture. I like to serve this in a baby food jar that is made by the company BÉABA. It has a great shape. Spoon the smooth marrow into the bottom of the jar and place a dollop of the crunchy bone bits on top. Serve with thin, grilled crostini, some salt, a lemon, pickled peppers, and hot sauce.

Ramp Tempura

Nate Allen

12 ramps
¾ cup White Lily self-rising
  flour
¾ cup cornstarch
1 teaspoon sugar
Pinch salt
Pinch black pepper
½ teaspoon cayenne
1 teaspoon fresh thyme leaves
12–16 ounces ice cold beer
Frying oil

Clean and rinse ramps. Shake off excess water and dredge quickly in cornstarch. Mix together all other ingredients (apart from frying oil) to form tempura batter, which should be like loose pancake batter. (The best way to tell if it is the right consistency is to dip your finger in cornstarch and then batter your finger tip. It should just barely stick, with bits dripping off.)

Heat oil to 350°F. Dip ramps one by one in tempura batter, allow excess to drip off, wave each back and forth 3 times in the oil (softly whispering how much you love it; it is very important to talk to the ramp!), then drop in entirely, and leave until batter is crunchy-crispy. Drain and serve hot with extra salt if desired.

Tomato Granita

John Fleer

Long-time executive chef at Blackberry Farm as well as Canyon Kitchen in Cashiers, and now at his own Rhubarb in Asheville, Chef Fleer is a gentle giant who works magic in the kitchen. This is a delightfully cooling summer appetizer which could serve just as well as a palate cleanser, or as a dessert.

1½ cups sugar
1 cup water
4 sprigs basil
2 pounds very ripe tomatoes (all of the same color and preferably the same variety), chopped
Pinch freshly cracked black pepper
½ teaspoon kosher salt
1 teaspoon lemon juice

Bring sugar and water to a boil. Simmer until all sugar is dissolved. Remove from heat and stir in basil sprigs to make basil "tea." Let cool for half an hour.

Place chopped tomatoes with all their juices in blender with pepper, lemon juice and salt. Blend until liquid. Pass through a fine sieve and push as many solids through the sieve as possible.

Remove basil stalks from simple syrup. Add syrup to tomato purée, testing for sweetness and flavor. Pour into a shallow pan in the freezer and stir every 20 minutes until crystals form and granité is achieved.

Pickled Pig Trotter with Roasted Sunchokes

Sarsaparilla Cream, Pine Nut Butter, Arugula, & Crispy Sumac   Serves 8

Edwin Bloodworth

I am an advocate of recipes containing three ingredients and as few steps as I can get by with, without compromising the deliciousness. There are, however, some recipes that just take time, and lots of it. For the ultra-ambitious, Chef Bloodworth has shared his recipe for Pickled Pig Trotters (with all the trimmings). You can generally find pig's feet in your local grocery, but if they are lacking, or are of questionable freshness, just address your butcher, or visit a farmer's market. Chef Bloodworth, like so many chefs in Asheville and environs, is focused on supporting local farmers and artisans, and exploring the wild foods the region has to offer, in an attempt to offer a "new form" of Appalachian cuisine.

For the Pickled Pig Trotter
2 trotters (split in half)

For the Curing Brine
500 grams (18 ounces/a little over 2 cups) water

500 grams (18 ounces/a little over 2 cups) ice

100 grams (3½ ounces, about ¼ cup) sugar

100 grams (3½ ounces, about ¼ cup) salt

10 grams (2 teaspoons) pink salt (optional for coloring)

Dissolve sugar and both salts in 500 grams of warm water. Add 500 grams of ice to chill. Vacuum seal the trotters in the brine and refrigerate for up to seven days. If you don't have a vacuum sealer, just put them in a Ziploc bag or a closed container with the brine.

For the Wild Sumac Pickling Liquid

500 grams (18 ounces/a little over 2 cups) white wine vinegar
500 grams (18 ounces/a little over 2 cups) water
300 grams (about 2 cups) sugar
200 grams (about 2 cups; sumac is lighter than sugar) dried sumac

Heat water, sugar, and sumac to a simmer. Cover and steep 1 hour. Strain and reserve liquid. Chill.

Remove trotters from the brine. Rinse well and vacuum seal with the pickling liquid. Cook the trotters at 180°F for 15 hours or until the meat can be pinched from the bone. (Alternatively, they could be braised in the oven at 225°F or 250°F, overnight, in a pan with the pickling liquid—or until the meat is easily picked from the bone.) Allow the trotters to rest for 20 minutes and then chill. Trotters can remain in the pickling liquid for up to one month.

Before serving, heat the trotters in the bags (or in the pickling liquid if not vacuum sealed). Remove and pick the meat and fat from the bones, trying to leave in large pieces. Each trotter half makes for two nice appetizer-sized portions. Reduce the pickling liquid and use to sauce the trotter after plating.

For the Roasted Sunchokes

16 medium-sized sunchokes, washed well
4 tablespoons grapeseed oil
6 grams (~1¼ teaspoons) salt
2 grams (~½ teaspoon) black pepper
4 grams (~¾ teaspoon) thyme sprigs

Toss sunchokes with grapeseed oil, salt, black pepper, and thyme. Roast in a covered pan for 30 min at 375°F or until desired tenderness is attained.

"Cooking is primarily fun...the more people know what they are doing, the more fun it is."
—JAMES BEARD

For the Sarsaparilla or Sassafras Cream*

250 grams (1 cup) half and half
250 grams (1 cup) heavy cream
40 grams (a little more than ⅛ cup) sugar
5 grams (~¾ teaspoon) sarsaparilla or dried sassafras root
2 grams (~½ teaspoon) salt
5 sheets of gelatin (silver)

Bring all to a simmer. Steep 20 minutes. Add gelatin. Strain into a ¼ sheet pan, lined with plastic wrap. Allow to set (may take up to two hours), and keep refrigerated.

For the Pine Nut Butter

250 grams (~1 cup) pine nuts, toasted
Sugar and salt to taste

Blend until smooth. Leave a few pine nuts whole to add additional texture to the dish.

"Cooking should be a carefully balanced reflection of all the good things of the earth."
—Jean and Pierre Troisgros

For the Crispy Sassafras Leaves

24 fresh sassafras leaves (smaller leaves are more tender and flavorful)

For the Leaf Brine

500 grams (18 ounces/a little over 2 cups) water
15 grams (3 teaspoons) salt

For the Simple Syrup

1000 grams (4¼ cups) water
500 grams (18 ounces/a little over 2 cups) sugar

Brine sassafras leaves for up to one week, then rinse. Simmer the leaves in simple syrup for 30 minutes. Move to dehydrator and leave until ready to use. Dehydrate at 140°F, for several hours, or until they crumble to the touch and melt in your mouth. If you don't have a dehydrator, place in a very low oven and keep close watch.

For the Arugula

Wash and choose the smallest and nicest of the arugula leaves. You will need at least 48 leaves (6 per plate). The spice of the arugula cuts the fat and balances the sweet elements of the dish.

To Plate

Place pine nut butter on the plate, lay sunchokes and trotter throughout the pine nut base, drizzle on sarsaparilla cream, finish with arugula and the crispy sassafras leaves on top.

*Author's Note: Sarsaparilla is derived from the dried roots of the tropical Smilax regelii, and is associated with a carbonated drink popular in the mid-1800s. Sassafras, from which root beer was created, is a lot more attainable, at least in Appalachian climes.

Ramp-Seasoned Morel Mushrooms with Egg Pasta

Mark Rosenstein

½ pound morel mushrooms,
  cleaned
4 tablespoons butter
1 tablespoon olive oil
½ teaspoon ramp seasoning
  (dried ramp leaves ground
  to a powder with a little salt)
¼ cup dry white wine
6 ounces fresh pasta
Grated Parmesan cheese
  to taste
Salt and pepper to taste

In a heavy skillet, over moderate heat, melt 2 tablespoons of the butter and the oil. Sauté the mushrooms for about 8 minutes, season with ramp seasoning, salt (go easy), and pepper. Add wine, lower heat, and cook slowly.

While the mushrooms are cooking, bring water to a boil and cook the pasta. Drain, toss into the mushrooms, add the remaining 2 tablespoons of butter, swirl, serve, and grate cheese over top.

Tennessee Ham-Wrapped Peaches
with Stracciatella, Toasted Hazelnuts, Bourbon Barrel Maple Syrup, Sorrel Serves 4

William Dissen

Chef Dissen has been in touch with nature and the outdoors ever since he was a child growing up in West Virginia, where he watched his grandmother cook bountiful meals straight from the garden. A huge advocate of sustainability, he strives to bring home the point that there can be no cuisine without gardens and farmers.

For the Peaches
5 peaches, ripe, cut into
    quarters, pit removed
20 slices Tennessee country
    ham (preferably Allan
    Benton's), sliced thin
2 tablespoons blended oil
    (75% olive, 25% vegetable)
Black pepper, ground, to taste

For the Stracciatella
2 cups mozzarella curd,
    large dice
1 cup heavy cream
1 gallon water
1 cup kosher salt

For the Hazelnuts
1 cup hazelnuts, blanched
¾ cup sugar
3 tablespoons water
½ teaspoon smoked paprika
½ teaspoon sea salt

For the Garnish
5 tablespoons bourbon barrel
    maple syrup (preferably from
    Bourbon Barrel Foods)
Red ribbon sorrel, as needed
Pea shoots, as needed
4 tablespoons extra virgin
    olive oil

For the Peaches

Wrap each peach quarter with 1 slice of country ham and reserve on a parchment-lined plate. Preheat a cast iron pan over medium heat with the blended oil. Place the slices into the pan. Sprinkle gently with ground black pepper, and cook for about 4–5 minutes, or until the ham is golden and crispy on one side. Turn the peaches, crispy side up, and place onto a paper towel-lined plate. Reserve.

For the Stracciatella

Place the water and salt into a medium pot and bring to a rapid boil. Place the diced mozzarella curd into the pot. Using a long metal slotted spoon, stir the curd until it just starts to melt on the edges. Quickly remove the curd from the pot and transfer to a large bowl, draining away as much water as possible. Allow to cool for 3–4 minutes. Working with your hands, shred the mozzarella curd into fine threads. Stir in the heavy cream and black pepper. The stracciatella should have the consistency of ricotta cheese. Taste, and adjust seasoning as needed. Reserve.

For the Hazelnuts

In a small pot, bring the sugar and water to a simmer over high heat, stirring to dissolve, until sugar mixture is amber in color (about 4–5 minutes). Remove the pan from the heat, add the smoked paprika, sea salt, and hazelnuts, and stir to evenly coat. Place candied hazelnuts on a sheet tray lined with a nonstick mat, and quickly separate using a spatula or a fork. Allow to cool. Once cool, place the hazelnuts into a food processor and pulse 3–4 times to lightly crumble the hazelnuts into chunks. Reserve.

For the Finish

Place a large spoonful of the stracciatella across the plate. Arrange the roasted ham-wrapped peaches over the stracciatella. Directly over each peach, place 1 teaspoon of the bourbon barrel maple syrup. Garnish each peach with pea shoots, red ribbon sorrel, and extra virgin olive oil. Sprinkle the hazelnuts around each peach and serve immediately.

Fried Green Tomatoes

SG Séguret

A staple of Southern Appalachian cuisine, this is a great way to use up those end-of-season tomatoes that refuse to ripen on the vine. Of course you can steal a green tomato at any time and fry it up early in the season as well. This is also good treatment for a winter supermarket tomato which would not otherwise have any flavor.

A couple of large green tomatoes
A few tablespoons cornmeal
Cajun seasoning ("Slap Ya
   Mama," if you can find it)
Oil for frying

Slice tomatoes and roll—or shake in a bag—with cornmeal and seasoning. (If you don't have any Cajun seasoning handy, combine salt, black pepper, cayenne, and dried or fresh crushed garlic.) Heat oil in skillet and fry until crispy on both sides. Serve hot as a side dish, an appetizer, or as a layer in a sandwich. This is a great way to dress up a burger, along with a little horseradish mayonnaise.

"When shopping for fruits and vegetables, use at least three senses: sight, touch, and smell."
—Dr. John LaPuma

Possum Paté

SG Séguret

A possum has nine lives. Once you get beyond that fact, the actual preparation is no more challenging than cooking up a rabbit, which can be substituted in this recipe if you don't get beyond the aforementioned fact, or if you are opposed to eating a marsupial. If you are opposed to the idea of eating a rabbit as well, try the same recipe with chicken morsels. It will be less tasty, but won't shock your guests.

1 possum (or 1 rabbit), skinned
   and cleaned
A couple of shallots
Dijon mustard
A few sprigs of thyme
A couple of bay leaves
A bottle of dry white wine
Salt and pepper to taste

Remove any silverskin (thin, silvery layer of connective tissue found between the skin and the flesh of wild game), excess fat, and visible glands from the meat, and cut into pieces as you would a rabbit (similar to cutting up a chicken). Sweat some chopped shallots in olive oil, in the bottom of a cast iron Dutch oven. Remove shallots while still translucent and set aside. Salt and pepper the possum pieces and sprinkle with fresh thyme leaves. Brown in olive oil in the Dutch oven. Brush possum pieces with mustard (only real Dijon will do), and sear again. Add a bottle of dry white wine and a few bay leaves, cover, and simmer for a couple of hours (2 will probably be sufficient, depending on the size and age of your possum).

At this point you can serve possum pieces with sweet potatoes and poke sallet (page 147) or collard greens (page 73), or, to get to the paté stage, you can continue simmering until the meat falls off the bones.

Pick all the meat off the bones with your fingers (be careful; there are many of them—bones, that is!), and pack in a small earthenware dish. Cover with a lid and refrigerate. When ready to serve, spread on toast and present as an hors d'oeuvre, garnished with wild mustard flowers.

From the Henhouse

Where the day begins bright and early

Written in 1944 by Andy Razaf and made popular by Phil Harris's 1947 RCA Victor recording, these classic lyrics sing of the just-as-classic ingredients we associate with Southern cuisine, many of which are Appalachian as well.

That's What I Like about the South

Andy Razaf

Won't you come with me to Alabamy
Let's go see my dear old Mammy
She's fryin' eggs and broiling hammy
That's what I like about the South

Now there you can make no
    mistakey
Where those nerves are never shaky
Ought to taste her layer cakey
That's what I like about the South

She's got baked ribs and candied
    yams
Those sugar-cured Virginia hams
Basement full of those berry jams
An' that's what I like about the
    South

Hot corn bread, black-eyed peas
You can eat as much as you please
'Cause it's never out of season
That's what I like about the South

Aahhh, don't take one, have two
There's dark brown and chocolate too
Suits me, they must suit you
'Cause that's what I like about the
    South

Well it's way, way down where the
    cane grows tall
Down where they say "Y'all"
Walk on in with that Southern drawl
'Cause that's what I like about the
    South

Down where they have those pretty
    queens
Keep a-dreamin' those dreamy
    dreams
Well let's sip that absinthe in New
    Orleans
That's what I like about the South

Here come old Bob with all the news
Got the boxback coat with button
    shoes

But he's all caught up with his union
   dues
An' that's what I like about the
   South

Here come old Roy down the street
Ho, can't you hear those tappin' feet
He would rather sleep than eat
An' that's what I like about the
   South

Now every time I pass your door
You act like you don't want me no
   more
Why don't you shake that head and
   sigh
And I'll go walkin' right on by

On, on, on
And on and on
Honey, when you tell me that you
   love me
Then how come you close your eyes

Did I tell you 'bout the place called
   Doo-wah-diddy
It ain't no town and it ain't no city
It's just awful small, but awful
   pretty
That's Doo-wah-diddy

Well I didn't come here to criticize
I'm not here to sympathize
But don't tell me those no-good lies
'Cause a lyin' gal I do despise

You love me like I love you
Send me fifty P-D-Q
Roses are red and violets are pink
I won't get all fifty, I don't think

She's got backbones and turnip
   greens
Ham hocks and butter beans
You, me and New Orleans
An' that's what I like about the
   South

"We know how to wisely dole out abundance, and when things aren't abundant, we know how to make the most of what we have. We see not only what is in our hands at the moment, but can envision how we'll need it later and in what form it can serve us best."
—SHERI CASTLE

Ramp & Morel Omelette

SG Séguret

Small handful of ramps
Large handful of morels
Fresh eggs, 2 per person
Splash of milk or cream
2 tablespoons (more or less)
    butter
Salt and pepper to taste

The French favor what is known as an "omelette baveuse," which literally means drooling omelette, or as one book of slang would have it, "dripping spittle omelette"! Once you have tried this, with a slightly crisped outside and a jiggly soft inside, you will likely never go back to your old dry version. Experiment until you find just the texture that pleases you!

Clean, slice, and sauté ramps, put butter and a smidgen of olive oil (or bacon fat) in a nonstick pan and sauté the whites of the ramps until translucent, then add the green part and sauté just until wilted.

Mix eggs, cream, salt, and pepper, and add to pan. Run nonstick spatula around the edges of the pan as omelette is cooking (on medium heat), lifting edges here and there, allowing uncooked part to run under the rest of the omelette. Continue until omelette is almost set, and still jiggly but not overly wet in the center.*

Turn up heat briefly to make sure bottom of omelette is cooked enough to fold without falling apart, but not so much that it will be dry and crack when folded. Fold in half in the pan, and turn out on warm platter.

Have morels ready, sliced and sautéed in butter until just beginning to crisp, and sprinkled with coarse salt. Top the omelette with the morels and melted butter, and serve immediately. Follow with a salad of fresh spring greens (watercress makes an excellent complement).

Baked Eggs in Cream

SG Séguret

Easy to prepare and quick to please, this is one of the simplest dishes ever, and the most satisfying. Try it with any number of variations, but don't forget to try the simple version first so that you can enjoy the fulsome flavor of the egg. This is my go-to dish when I am writing and suddenly realize I have forgotten to eat. In 10 minutes, with no sweat, I have a miniature feast to warm the stomach and feed the brain.

Fresh farm eggs, 1 per ramekin
  (1 or 2 per person)
Heavy cream (~1 teaspoon to
  cover each egg)
Butter to line each ramekin
Salt and pepper to taste

Butter a ramekin (one or two per person, depending on the placement in the meal). Break an egg in each ramekin, being careful to leave the yolk intact. Pour a little heavy cream (about a teaspoonful) over each yolk. Grind a bit of pepper and sprinkle with a few grains of sea salt. Put in the oven (400°F) for 8 minutes, depending on the size of your eggs. Pour yourself something to drink, and relax.

This can be an appetizer, a pick-me-up, a breakfast component, or a before-bed snack. Try garnishing with chopped tarragon or sorrel or any one or combination of your favorite herbs. Or garnish with sautéed mushrooms or bits of leftover bacon from breakfast. Throw in a few hot pepper flakes for some bite, or some sautéed ramps or daylily buds. Be inventive.

Ramped-Up Deviled Eggs

SG Séguret

Fresh farm eggs, 1 or 2 per
  person
Heavy cream, enough to
  moisten yolks
Several ramps
Dijon mustard to taste
Salt and pepper to taste

*"Omne vivum ex ovo
(All life comes from an egg)."*
—Latin proverb

Hard boil a bunch of eggs (leftovers
are always welcome!), being sure not
to over-cook (a scant 8–10 minutes
is plenty). Cool, peel, and halve,
scooping out the centers. Clean
and fine-chop a few ramps, leaves
included, and mix them in with the
yolks, along with a good dollop of
Dijon mustard and cream to the right
consistency. Add salt and pepper to
taste. Fill the whites and garnish, if
you wish, with salted capers. Enjoy!

If ramps are not to your palate,
chop up some fresh basil, or any
other herb, or yet again some spring
onions, and use in place of the ramps.

Ramp & Nettle Quiche

SG Séguret

I am fortunate to have always lived with ramps and nettles out my back door. The below is my adaptation of a classic French quiche Lorraine recipe minus the bacon and cheese! (The French would use crème fraiche in place of sour cream, but either one works beautifully.) The crust is one imparted to me by a 90-year-old French countrywoman, who, like the old woman in the shoe, had so many (grand)children she didn't know what to do. So she made endless pies. Her simple two-minute recipe, using a spoon and a fork and a bowl and fingers, completely transformed my life and has made pies (both sweet and savory), tarts, and pizzas an easy anyday occurrence in my household.

4 large eggs

1 large container (16 ounces) of sour cream

Grating of fresh nutmeg

Salt and pepper to taste

10 rounded spoonfuls of all-purpose flour

5 spoonfuls of oil

5 spoonfuls of water

Bunch of ramps

Bucketful of nettles

Dig your ramps selectively, leaving a few in each clump in the wild, wash and trim, and return the roots to the woods where they can take life again. Slice ramps in small rounds, using the leaves as well, and sauté lightly in butter or bacon fat.

Gather a pail of nettles (use a dish glove to keep the sting from afflicting you), wash them a couple of times to cull insects and other creatures, and wilt in a large pot with just a little water until more ruly but still bright green. Drain and chop.

Spoon 10 rounded soupspoons (serving spoon size; approximately 1 rounded tablespoon) full of flour into a mixing bowl, add 5 level spoonfuls of oil (either olive or safflower, or oil of choice), and 5 level spoonfuls of water, a small palmful of large-grained salt, and chopped herbs (rosemary and/ or thyme or oregano) if desired. Stir around rapidly with a fork, form a ball, and pat out into your 10-inch pie dish, making sure the dough is an even thickness in all places, particularly in the corners. The dough, from start to finish, takes about two minutes (plus a little more if you are gathering and chopping herbs).

Whisk four eggs, fresh from your henhouse if possible, with a pot of sour cream and add a grinding of pepper and salt and another few grindings of fresh nutmeg. Spread sautéed ramps and chopped nettles on the unbaked pie crust, top with custard, and bake at 400°F for 30 minutes. Serve with a bright, crisp white wine (or chilled sassafras tea) and a salad of fresh spring greens.

Ramp Mayonnaise

SG Séguret

If you've never made your own mayonnaise, it's high time you got started. Nothing could be more simple, and the freshness is beyond comparison with store bought varieties. For plain mayonnaise, omit the ramp. For classic aioli, replace ramp with finely chopped garlic. For herbed mayonnaise, add finely chopped herbs of choice (tarragon, dill, oregano, thyme, sorrel, basil…)

1 egg yolk
½ teaspoon Dijon mustard
1 finely chopped ramp
Olive oil to taste
Salt to taste

Separate yolk from white, and save white for another purpose. Put the Dijon mustard in the bottom of an ample bowl with the egg yolk. Turn rapidly with a whisk and, still whisking, add a slow, steady stream of olive oil until you've reached your desired consistency. Add the chopped ramps, salt to taste, and consume within the next three or four days.

From the Garden

A rainbow of colors to dress your plate

Written by Madison County, North Carolina, native Marty Lewis, several of whose recipes appear in this chapter, this delightful treatise to the important things of life can be heard on a 2003 recording for Root Records, called Mountain Boys. Having grown up myself on Tater Gap Road, this song holds a particular resonance.

Tater Patch

Marty Lewis

Bye-bye 'tater patch, hello city life
No more corn and 'maters, now, I've
took a city wife
No more okra or sweet peas, does she
mean that much to me
Bye-bye 'tater patch, hello city life

Workin' in the garden almost every
day
Mowin' and a-tillin', tryin' to keep
the weeds away
She said the garden has to go, can I
do it, I don't know
Bye-bye 'tater patch, hello city life

Bye-bye 'tater patch, hello city life
No more corn and maters, now, I've
took a city wife

No more okra or sweet peas, does she
mean that much to me
Bye-bye 'tater patch, hello city life

Well, she don't like cornbread or
onions with her beans
But our love together is the best
you've ever seen
No more mule out in the stall, throw
away those overalls
Bye-bye 'tater patch, hello city life

Bye-bye 'tater patch, hello city life
No more corn and maters, now, I've
took a city wife
No more okra or sweet peas, does she
mean that much to me
Bye-bye 'tater patch, hello city life

Stack of Early Summer Tomato Salad with Avocado Mash

James Boyce

For the Salad

4 ripe tomatoes

2 shallots

1 tablespoon minced chives

2 tablespoons extra virgin
    olive oil

2 tablespoons minced fennel

Salt and pepper to taste

For the Avocado Mash

1 ripe avocado

1 grapefruit, sectioned

1 tablespoon lemon juice

2 teaspoons chives, chopped

2 tablespoons extra virgin
    olive oil

Salt and pepper to taste

Wash tomatoes and slice as thinly as possible. Lay on a platter and sprinkle with shallots, chives, olive oil, fennel, and pepper. Allow to marinate for 30 minutes.

With a fork, roughly mash the avocado and add remaining ingredients. Season to taste.

Presentation

Layer the tomatoes with the avocado and grapefruit mash, and top with crunchy salt and mixed field greens.

Kilt Lettuce

Marty Lewis

Some of the best recipes of all time require little sweat and few ingredients, but yield just as much satisfaction as more complicated ones. Marty excels at the backbone of Southern Appalachian recipes, often learned from his father, and travels with a skillet in the back of his truck, ready to whip up a feast wherever there is famine.

A couple heads of green leaf
    lettuce
2 tablespoons bacon grease
Salt to taste

Get a skillet going until it sizzles when you flick a drop of water on it. Add bacon grease, add washed greens (whole leaves), turn until wilted (kilt) and tender, and serve piping hot.

Fried Cabbage

Marty Lewis

1 big cabbage head
2 tablespoons olive oil
Salt and black pepper to taste
Cayenne pepper flakes to taste

Slice cabbage in strands, heat skillet to medium-high, add oil, then cabbage and black pepper and a little salt. Sauté until tender but firm, and sprinkle with cayenne. Serve with pork chops and cornbread, or just as is.

Rattlesnake Beans with Mushrooms & Thyme-Infused Honey

Mary Collins-Shepard

In 2014, the Seasonal School of Culinary Arts held a special day devoted to cooking with honey, in honor of Laurey Masterton, iconic Asheville chef and caterer and bee keeper. When Mary mentioned to the Warren Wilson garden manager that she needed beans and mushrooms for her class on cooking with honey, he came back with several pounds of "rattlesnake" pole beans, shiitakes and cremini mushrooms. This recipe, as well as appearing in the 2014 Seasonal School of Culinary Arts Cookbook, was featured in Debby Maugans' and Christine Sykes Lowe's Farmer & Chef Asheville. A drizzle of thyme-infused honey gives a kiss of sweetness to the quick-cooked fresh vegetables.

For the Honey

¾ cup local honey

4 generous sprigs thyme

¼ teaspoon sea salt

For the Vegetables

1½ pounds fresh "rattlesnake"
    or other green beans

8 ounces mixed fresh
    mushrooms (shiitake,
    cremini, oyster), sliced

3 tablespoons unsalted butter

2 medium shallots, thinly sliced

¼ teaspoon sea salt, or to taste

¼ teaspoon freshly ground
    pepper, or to taste

Warm the honey to just below a simmer in a small saucepan over medium heat. Remove from the heat and stir in the thyme and salt. Cover and let stand at least 1 hour.

Remove any strings from the beans, if necessary. Snap the beans in half if they are long (over 4 inches). Cook the beans in a large saucepan of boiling, salted water until they are crisp-tender, 3 to 4 minutes. Drain and place in a large bowl of ice water to stop cooking. Drain again and pat dry.

Remove the thyme stems from the infused honey (the leaves can stay), and place over low heat to warm.

Place a large, heavy skillet over medium-high heat. Add the butter and let it melt. Add the shallots and sauté until they are translucent, about 2 minutes. Add the mushrooms and sauté until just tender, about 4 minutes. Add the blanched beans and cook, stirring occasionally until they are hot, about 5 minutes. Transfer to a bowl and drizzle with the honey.

Half Runners & Greasy Cut-Shorts

Marty Lewis

Generous portion half runners*, strung and bobbed (tips and tails removed)
Equal portion greasy Cut-Shorts*, also strung and bobbed
Palmful of salt
Slab of side meat (salt pork)
Half a dozen to a dozen new potatoes
Little pinch of sugar (optional)

For heirloom bean descriptions, see page 195.

Throw beans (good Southern beans found at the farmers market; can use one or both varieties) in great big pot, cover generously with water, add side meat, salt, and sugar, bring to a boil, turn down heat, and simmer. Drop new potatoes in the pot (up to 3 per person) for an extra treat. Cook up to an hour until bean almost changes color from dark green to light green. Serve with slotted spoon, accompanied by fresh garden onions, pork chop, cornbread, sliced cucumber, and country chow-chow.

Roasted Beet Salad

Joe Scully

I have never been a fan of beets, which were an all-too-regular part of my childhood summer diet, and always smacked a bit too much of dirt for my taste. Despite the delectability of baby beets, I feel the best treatment of a beet is to soak it in bourbon, wrap it in bacon, drizzle it in butter, sprinkle it in thyme, and roast it until the bacon crisps up. Or feed it to the chickens. Joe has another idea which is sure to appeal to the majority of beet lovers and beet haters alike.

5 pounds purple beets
1 red onion
½ cup vegetable oil
1½ cups sugar
1½ cups apple cider vinegar
Salt and pepper to taste

Preheat oven to 350°F. Toss the beets in vegetable oil, season with salt and pepper and place in roasting pan. Cover the pan with a lid and roast for 2½ hours. Remove from roasting pan while still hot and place in another container. Wrap entire container tight with plastic wrap and let cool for an hour or more. Once cool, use a wet dish towel and rub the skins off of the beets. Julienne the beets on a mandolin with the wide blade attachment (or with a knife) and place in a mixing bowl. Julienne the red onion and place in the bowl with beets. Season the beets with apple cider vinegar, sugar, salt and pepper. Add vegetable oil to give them a nice sheen. You are looking for the balance in flavor of tart and sweet.

For the Garnish

2 pounds golden beets

2 cups sugar

2 cups apple cider vinegar

Salt and pepper to taste

Julienne the beets on a mandolin with the medium blade attachment (or with a knife) and place in sauce pot. Add sugar, vinegar, salt, and pepper. Bring to a boil and then simmer for 5 to 10 minutes until beets are beginning to get tender. Strain the beets and reserve the liquid. Cool the beets and then place back in the pickling liquid.

Presentation Note

Serve the purple beet salad in a bowl or on a platter with the pickled golden beets on top. It is nice to use arugula or baby spinach as a base to keep the beet juice from running on the plate.

Red Cabbage Slaw

Joe Scully

1 head red cabbage

⅓ cup cane sugar

½ cup apple cider vinegar

¾ cup salad oil

1 bulb roasted garlic (mashed into paste)

Salt and pepper to taste

Core and slice the red cabbage on the mandolin, or with a good knife (very fine). Toss with everything else. Season to taste.

Early Fall Succotash

Joe Scully

Chef Scully's two flagship Asheville restaurants, Corner Kitchen and Chestnut, reflect a maturing of the food scene in the mountains of Western North Carolina, coupled with "come as you are" service. Beyond the food, a moment of basking in Joe's warm smile is worth the price of the meal. This is a reminder of why so many of us cherish the memory of our grandmother's cooking. The greatest nourishment we can be given comes from the person who is feeding us, if that person is offering love on a plate.

½ pound corn, cut from the cob

½ pound butterbeans

½ pound okra

½ pound Crowder peas*

½ pound tomatoes, diced

2 yellow onions

4 potatoes, peeled and shredded

2 tablespoons garlic, chopped

1 pound butter

Tabasco to taste

Salt and pepper to taste

Note: The vegetables in this succotash can vary depending on what is left from your summer gardens after you have done all your canning and freezing for the winter.

Sauté the onions and garlic in 2 ounces of butter. Add the Crowder peas and cover with water. Cook for 10 minutes on high heat. Then add the butterbeans and cook for 10 minutes. Then add the okra, corn, and tomatoes and cook for 10 minutes. Continue to add water as needed to keep from scorching. Once all the vegetables are close to being tender, add the shredded potatoes, Tabasco, and seasoning. Cook for several more minutes until potatoes slightly thicken the mixture. Finish with the butter. The succotash should be rich and hearty with lots of tender vegetables.

*Author's Note: Field peas, crowder peas, cream peas, and black-eyed peas are all part of a larger species of beans commonly called "cowpeas" or "Southern peas." Despite their names, these varieties are actually technically beans (Vigna unguiculata) rather than peas. They were brought to the New World from Africa and became part of the Southern diet as early as the 1600s. Cowpeas are prevalent in the South because they are adaptable, heat-tolerant, and drought-resistant. The crowder pea variety gets its name from the way the seeds crowd themselves in the pod.

Chestnut Sweet Potato Salad

Joe Scully

1 gallon sweet potatoes, peeled
   and cut into ¾-inch dice
2 red onions, diced
3 green peppers, diced
3 red peppers, diced
1 cup stone ground mustard
¾ cup chives, (chopped fine)
1 cup cider vinegar
1½–2 cups olive oil
Salt and pepper to taste

Heat oven to 350°F. Prepare all the vegetables. Toss the sweet potatoes in a little of the olive oil and oven roast until cooked. Toss the peppers and onion in a little olive oil as well and oven wilt them. While still warm, toss the peppers, onion, sweet potatoes, and mustard together, add cider vinegar. Season to taste and finish with the chives.

Susi's Jack Daniels-Infused Collards

SG Séguret

I was raised with steamed greens—spinach, chard, nettles, beet greens—and, fresh and wonderful as they may have been, I always felt there was something that might make them even tastier. Enter bacon fat and Jack Daniels, and the odd cracklin', and listen to those taste buds sing!

Several bunches collard greens

A few tablespoons bacon fat or olive oil

Several garlic cloves

Vinegar to taste

Broth (optional) for extra moistening (can also use water)

Hot chipotle pepper flakes to taste

Coarse-grain salt to taste

Fresh ground pepper to taste

Jack Daniels to taste

A few tablespoons of cracklin's to garnish (optional)

Wash and de-stem collards. Heat fat and sweat slivered garlic. Chop collards into half-inch ribbons and add to the hot skillet (a wok works well here too). Add salt, pepper, and pepper flakes, and wilt slightly. Add a couple of splashes of vinegar and evaporate slightly. Add broth (enough to keep from going dry, but not enough to turn soupy; water can be used here if you don't have broth, but the broth will give your dish more depth), cover, and simmer until desired tenderness is reached (less time will turn out chewy collards, which some may prefer; more time will turn out collards that melt in your mouth). Add a splash or two of Jack Daniels (pour yourself some to sip too!), and simmer a moment longer.

Serve atop grits or alongside pork chops or as a garnish for soupbeans, or in a bowl with the potlikker for a one-pot-dish with some cornbread on the side. Crispy sautéed cracklin's to top off the bowl will take you over the top!

Denny's Appalachian-Style Collard Greens

Denny Trantham

Denny, true to his Appalachian roots, carries a jar of bacon grease with him everywhere he goes and doesn't use it lightly. I think if he were ever to find himself in any kind of conflict, be it domestic or international, all he would have to do would be to whip out his bacon fat and he could grease his way out of the stickiest situation. But Denny, being the Southern gentleman he is, does not even have to whip out his bacon grease for reconciliation, so all of it is left to go in his rich and heady dishes.

12 hickory-smoked bacon slices, finely chopped

2 medium-sized sweet onions, finely chopped

¾ pound smoked ham, chopped

6 garlic cloves, finely chopped

3 (32-ounce) containers chicken broth

3 (1-pound) packages fresh collard greens, washed and trimmed

8 ounces bacon grease

½ cup apple cider vinegar

1 tablespoon ground mustard

1 tablespoon crushed red pepper

1 tablespoon sugar

1 teaspoon salt

¾ teaspoon black pepper

Cook bacon in a 10-quart stockpot over medium heat 10 to 12 minutes or until almost crisp. Add onion and sauté 8 minutes; add ham and garlic and sauté 1 minute. Stir in broth and all remaining ingredients. Cook 3 hours or to desired degree of tenderness.

Aromatic Vegetables in a Paper Bag

Serves 8

John Fleer

½ cup extra virgin olive oil

1 pound carrots (preferably
with tops)

1 pound baby leeks, scallions
or ramps

3 cloves garlic, sliced (can also
use green garlic or garlic
scapes)

1 pound celery with leaves

8 sprigs thyme

8 leaves basil

Salt and pepper to taste

Cut vegetables so that they will cook at basically the same rate. In a bowl, toss vegetables with olive oil, salt, and pepper. Divide vegetables among 8 paper bags. Add a sprig of thyme and a basil leaf to each bag. Roll top of bag and place on a sheet pan. Bag will be a bit oily. That's ok. Roast at 375°F until vegetables are just soft. Bring bag still sealed to the table and allow diner to experience the aroma of the opening bag.

Note: Other vegetables can be substituted—do not use cruciferous vegetables (cabbage/broccoli) or high water content vegetables (tomatoes/summer squash).

Barbecued Shelly Beans

Polly Gott

My mother is a whiz in the kitchen, coming in from a long day in the garden or a long day watercolor painting (often whipping off 10 masterpieces in the course of a few hours), and putting dinner on the table in a matter of a scant half hour, including building the fire for the wood cookstove and carrying water in earlier days. Most of her meals of my childhood consisted of steamed, boiled, or fried vegetables in various combinations—corn, beans, and  *'taters; or beans, 'taters, and corn—you get the picture. Exceptionally, she would prepare barbecued soy beans, from the dried soy beans that helped us get through the winter, as we made a trip to the supermarket only twice a year. She served them with potatoes grown on our farm and baked in squares of foil, buried in the hot ashes of the fireplace. This was fancy fare, and always a rare treat. She has since replaced the soy beans with Shelly beans, but the recipe can be executed with any type of dried bean, once cooked.*

¼ cup oil

3 medium onions

3 cloves garlic, crushed

1 quart tomatoes (home-canned or fresh)

¼ cup molasses

2 tablespoons soy sauce

½ teaspoon allspice

2 teaspoons salt

1–2 fresh hot peppers (or 1 dried hot pepper)

¼ cup vinegar or ½ cup lemon juice

4 cups Shelly beans, cooked and drained

Sauté onion and garlic over low heat in oil. Add tomatoes and stir well. Add molasses, soy sauce, allspice, salt, hot peppers, vinegar, and garlic. Bring to a boil and reduce to a simmer. Cook 15 minutes, then add drained beans and stir. Cook for another 15–20 minutes, letting the beans and sauce meld together so that the sauce flavor permeates the beans. Serve with baked potato, butter, and salt.

Warm Cabbage Salad
with Walnuts, Spinning Spider Goat Cheese and Benton's Country Ham

Mark Rosenstein

1 head red cabbage
8 slices bacon, pancetta or
   country ham
8 slices of 3-inch-long croutons,
   rubbed with garlic
½ cup toasted walnuts, or half
   English walnuts, half black
   walnuts or hazelnuts
2 tablespoons walnut vinegar
¼ cup duck fat*
4 one-ounce rounds goat cheese
1 tablespoon chopped parsley
Salt and pepper to taste

Chiffonade the cabbage. Bake the bacon (or ham) until crisp. Make croutons (cut in 3-inch-long strips for added elegance), rub with garlic.

Just before cooking, toss the cabbage with vinegar, and season with salt and pepper. Drain if necessary. Heat the duck fat in an iron skillet over medium-high heat. Add the cabbage and cook rapidly for about 45 seconds. Add walnuts or hazelnuts. Toss, cook another minute. Garnish the plate with the bacon or ham and the croutons. Plate the cabbage, top with goat cheese round, and sprinkle with parsley.

Author's Note: Anything with duck fat is over-the-top delicious. If you don't have ducks in your backyard from which to render the fat, you can order a jar of duckfat from Farm Fresh Duck, from d'Artagnan, or even from Amazon.

Three Sisters Chowder

SG Séguret

This soup, born of the three staple ingredients of the early American's diet (corn, beans, squash) is excellent on a cold autumn day, or even on a hot summer day. Serve it in decorative bowls or in a hollowed-out pumpkin.

1 small pumpkin or winter squash, or a couple of yellow crooknecks during summertime

A few ears of corn, on or off the cob

A handful of fresh Shelly beans, or cooked dried beans or field peas (optional)

A couple potatoes

1–2 onions

Celery, a few ribs or to taste

Butter or olive oil to sauté vegetables

Fresh sage

1–3 bay leaves

Dash of cayenne

Chicken broth to cover ingredients

Heavy cream to finish off

Salt and pepper to taste

Chop an onion or two, depending on its size and on how many you are feeding, into a dice about the size of a large kernel of corn (~¼ inch). Sauté until translucent while similarly dicing your choice of squash. If using corn on the cob, remove the kernels and scrape the milk out of the cob with the back of your knife. Dice a few ribs of celery and add to the onions. Add broth, the potatoes, and winter squash or pumpkin dice, corn, salt and pepper, bay leaf, and sage chiffonade. (If making the summer version with yellow crookneck, wait until the last 10 minutes to add squash, or it will disintegrate and the prerequisite crunch will be absent.) Add the corn. Simmer until potatoes are tender. Season to taste, and finish off with heavy cream to the level of creaminess desired by you, the chef.

Creamed Swiss Chard & Corn

Jason Roy

Chef Roy, owner of Asheville's beloved Biscuit Head, is an innovative powerhouse who welcomes all with his infectious smile as he does things with biscuits that no one else would dare think about! The following recipe is a deviation from the classic succotash, confected with corn and lima beans.

1 large bunch Swiss chard,
   cleaned and cut
2 large ears local sweet corn,
   cut off the cob
1 clove garlic, minced
1 small sweet onion, diced
1 tablespoon olive oil
1 pint heavy whipping cream
Salt and pepper to taste

Heat a large sauté pan over medium-high heat. Add oil once the pan is hot, then add minced garlic and brown slightly. Add corn and onion, and stir for 45 seconds. Next, add the Swiss chard and sauté until chard is wilted. Finish with the heavy cream and simmer until cream has thickened into a velvety sauce that coats the vegetables. Season with salt and pepper. You can add some herbs from your garden if you desire; I like thyme with corn and chard.

Leeky Smashed Potatoes

John Fleer

This recipe could, of course, be done with ramps or spring onions in place of the leeks!

1 bunch leeks, white parts cut in
   half moons, washed
4 ounces butter
½ cup white wine
8 Red Bliss potatoes, about 4
   ounces each
¼ cup red wine vinegar
1 bay leaf
½ teaspoon black peppercorns
Kosher salt, a tablespoon or so
Finishing salt to taste

Melt butter in a sauté pan. Stir in leeks, season with salt, and sweat gently. Stir in white wine and continue to cook until fully soft.

Put potatoes in a large saucepot. Cover with cold water. Add vinegar, bay leaf, peppercorns, and kosher salt. Bring to a boil. Reduce the heat to a simmer for 12–15 minutes until potatoes are just tender. Drain and allow to cool briefly. Do not allow to cool completely. Place a potato on a clean cloth. Cover with another cloth and gently press/smash the potato. Repeat with remaining potatoes. Press a tablespoon of leeks onto each potato. Sear potatoes in a hot cast iron pan with olive oil. Serve as a side dish or as an appetizer on a bed of salad greens.

From the Woods

The deep, the dark, the mysterious

As previously noted, I grew up in a garden, surrounded by gardens, eating gardens, and also eating anything that ate the gardens. This song was one of my daddy's favorites, and I will always hear his banjo ring and his gleeful emphasis of the last "Groundhog!" at the end of each verse.

Groundhog

(Traditional)

Whet up your axe and whistle up
    your dog
We're off to the holler, gonna catch a
    groundhog
We're off to the woods to hunt
    groundhog
Groundhog!

Old Joe Digger, Sam, and Dave...
Went a-hog-huntin' just as hard as
    they could stave...

Too many rocks and too many logs...
Too many rocks for the catch a
    groundhog

Here comes Sam with a 10-foot
    pole...
Gonna roust that whistle pig outa
    his hole...

He's in here boys, the hole's wore
    slick...
Run here Sam with your forked
    stick...

Well, stand back, boys and let's be
    wise...
I think I see his beaded eyes...

Here he comes all in a whirl...
He's the biggest groundhog in this
    world...

Grab him by the tail and pull him
    out...
Great God almighty ain't a ground-
    hog stout...

Work, boys, work as hard as you can
    tear...
The meat'll do to eat and the hide'll
    do to wear...

Skin him out and tan his hide...
Best dern shoestrings ever I tied...

Well, the meat's in the pot, and the
    hide's in the churn...
If that ain't groundhog, I'll be
    durned...

The children scream, the children
    cry...
They love that groundhog cooked and
    fried...

I love my groundhog stewed and
    fried...
Little piece of cornbread by the
    side...

Hello, Mama, make Sam quit...
He's eatin' all the hog and don't leave
    me a bit...

Hello, boys, ain't it a sin...
Watch that gravy run down Sam's
    chin...

Watch him boys, he's about to fall...
He's et till his pants won't button
    at all...

Yonder comes Sal with a snigger and
    a grin...
Groundhog grease all over her chin...

"When I think about Appalachian food, it's about adapting, adapting to the land, social circumstances, environmental circumstances, it's always about adapting, evolving and moving forward."
—TRAVIS MILTON

Venison Ramp Meatloaf

Marty Lewis

Here's a recipe to make a mountain girl swoon! Of course it helps if the venison and hogmeat are from next door and if the ramps are freshly dug. In the absence of venison, use lean beef or buffalo, and in the absence of ramps use lots of spring onions and garlic. Try to hold out for the real thing at least once in your life.

1 pound ground venison
1 pound pork sausage
4 pieces white bread, dipped
   slightly in water
2 eggs
1 tablespoon salt
Liberal amount of pepper
Medium bunch chopped ramps
Lawry's seasoning (or
   sprinkling of paprika and/or
   turmeric)

Heat oven to 400°F. Oil generous glass or ceramic baking dish. Combine ingredients with your hands (directly in baking dish), kneading well, and pat out in a loaf, leaving a bit of room around the edges. Bake at 400°F for 34 minutes [sic], baste with any fat found around the edges, and continue baking another 34 minutes until crust forms on top. If more crusting is desired, turn on broiler for a scant 6 minutes (no watching TV!). Serve with mashed potatoes and kilt lettuce and cornbread and cold milk (or best selection from local brewery).

Nettle Soup

SG Séguret

During my young years, my mother served stinging nettles, wilted with butter and salt, as an early spring green. Unfortunately, she believed in keeping all the bugs and other creatures that inhabited the leaves (it was good protein and, since we carried water from a stream below, saved a step), and one of my early memories is of crunching on worm heads or finding a still white body lying within the folds of the leaves. We were not allowed to leave  *anything on our plates, so I bravely swallowed, but for a long time I was wary of nettles. When I moved to France for a 20-year spell, the centuries-old barnyard where I relocated was filled with nettles and not much else. I had few funds to buy fancy fare, so decided to tame them in a pot. The addition of onions and potatoes, and the simple act of puréeing, removed all fear of crunching on worm heads (it must also be said that I washed them religiously), and I fell in love with nettles for the first time.*

Large pailful of nettles
A couple potatoes
1 large or 2 small onions
Broth to cover
Several slices old bread
A couple tablespoons butter
Salt and pepper to taste
Heavy cream to swirl at end

Gather (with gloves) and wash a large pailful of nettles. Peel and dice an onion, and sauté it with a few diced potatoes (skin on if organic; peeled if not). Add homemade chicken broth (frozen is fine) and nettles, and cook until potatoes are soft and nettles wilted. Purée with an immersion blender, pour in soup bowls, garnish with a dollop of heavy cream, and swirl around with a knife tip to create interesting patterns. Top with freshly crisped croutons made from diced hunks of country-style bread sautéed in butter and salted.

Ramps, Smoked Bacon, & Arugula Salad Serves 4

Mark Rosenstein

2 ounces bacon, cut into lardons
(fat, short "sticks" about
¼ x ¼ x 1-inch)
Healthy bunch of ramps,
properly harvested, cleaned,
and cut into 1-inch lengths
1 teaspoon brown sugar
1 tablespoon apple cider vinegar
4 handfuls of fresh arugula
Salt and pepper to taste

In a heavy iron skillet over medium heat, cook the bacon until it renders its fat and becomes crispy. Toss in the ramps and cook for 1 minute, season with salt, pepper, and the brown sugar. Cook another minute. Add the vinegar and turn off the heat. Place the arugula in a mixing bowl, toss with the ramp and bacon dressing. Serve with some corn pone or corn bread sticks.

Wood-Grilled Hanger Steak
with Grilled Ramps and Morel Mushrooms
Serves 4

Mark Rosenstein

Ramps and morels, morels and ramps, ramps and ramps, morels and morels. Serve them with everything, until the season is gone! —M. Rosenstein

24 ounces beef hanger steak, brushed with oil, and well-seasoned with salt and pepper

2 handfuls of ramps, left whole, soaked in a little safflower oil and drained

Handful of fresh morels, brushed clean

Big bowl of fresh spinach or other spring green

2 tablespoons butter

1 whole lemon

Olive oil, enough to coat spinach

Salt and pepper to taste

Get the wood grill properly heated. Mix some 'shine & branch (moonshine and branch water!) together in a jar and sip while tending the fire. Have enough space on the grill to heat a small iron skillet as well. When the fire is ready, cook the meat properly, remembering to allow some time for it to rest before slicing. Halfway through, toss the ramps on the grill, season with some salt and pepper, cook them to a good char, and set aside on a warm plate. In the iron skillet, heat the butter until it foams, then cook the morels. Season with salt and pepper. Keep warm. Just as the meat is done, squeeze the lemon over the meat and set on a warm plate to rest. While the meat is resting, toss the spinach with olive oil, season with salt and pepper and toss it on the grill. (It will get a nice smoky flavor.) Let it char a bit, and return it to the bowl.

To serve, slice the hanger steak, return to the heated platter, and garnish with the ramps. Let people serve themselves. Refresh your jars.

Note: For this recipe, choose a wood-fired grill. If you choose to use gas, you might as well cook in a skillet.

Corn Grit Loaf with Ramps & Black Walnuts

Mark Rosenstein

3 ounces smoky bacon, cut into
  lardons
2 handfuls of fresh ramps,
  cleaned and wood grilled
½ cup black walnuts, coarsely
  chopped
1 cup baby turnips, roasted
Greens from the baby turnips,
  grilled and drained
Salt and pepper to taste

Equipment
1½ quart loaf-shaped mold
Oil to coat mold

First, assemble all the ingredients. Cook corn grits to yield 4 cups. Grill the ramps and the turnip greens (wash the greens in three changes of water and dry well). To grill them, toss each separately in oil and grill to desired doneness. Place in a colander to drain. Cook the bacon until crispy, reserving the rendered fat for another use. Toss the black walnuts in with the bacon during the last minute or two, to crisp (be careful not to burn). Drain the bacon and nuts in a colander. Roast the turnips until tender and cut into quarters. Season everything well.

To assemble, oil the loaf mold. If you like, line it with a piece of oiled baking paper to facilitate unmolding later. Heat the grits just until warm and softened. Place a half-inch layer of grits on the bottom of the mold, then lay in some ramps, turnip greens, bacon, and walnuts. Add more grits and repeat the layering, finishing the top with grits. Smooth the top and place a piece of oiled baking paper on top. Place a weight on top of that. Refrigerate for at least six hours.

Unmold and serve. You may serve it cold, or I prefer cutting the loaf into slices and cooking them very slowly in some fat until it's crispy on both sides. Serve with some very finely cut slaw or early spring greens, tossed with a little dressing.

Roasted Leg of Venison

SG Séguret

In the absence of venison, this recipe can be carried out well with a leg of lamb.

1 hindquarter or shoulder of
    venison
2 heads garlic
Handful of rosemary
Handful of thyme
Generous quantity large grain
    salt
Lots of freshly ground pepper
Olive oil to bind

Note: You can replace the garlic with finely chopped ramps for an even woodsier taste.

Trim off any silverskin and excessive fat (there will not be much of the latter, venison being a lean meat, but there may be a lot of the former). Make a paste from the crushed garlic (I save time by using a Zyliss garlic press, which is strong enough so that you don't even have to peel the clove; the skin remains in the press, and I scrape it out with a fork between each pressing), the chopped thyme, and rosemary, enough large-grain salt to effectively season the leg but not so much that it will be overly salty, a generous dose of freshly ground pepper, and enough olive oil to bind it all together.

Spread the paste over the leg and bake it in a 400°F oven, much as you would a leg of lamb. Timing will be anywhere from 45 minutes to an hour and a half, depending on the size of the leg. You want the meat to be rosy, as you would duck or lamb. It should resemble a rare roast beef when sliced.

Venison Country-Style Steak

Marty Lewis

Country-style, also called chicken-fried steak, is a great way to utilize steak cuts which might otherwise be too tough for the common palate. Dredged in flour and spices like fried chicken and then covered in gravy and cooked long and slow in the oven until tender through and through, the gravy can and should almost stand on its own.

1 "cube steak" per person
1 cup (more or less) flour
A couple tablespoons olive oil
1–2 onions
1 quart beef broth to cover
Handful of herbs if handy
Salt and pepper to taste

Cook onions in olive oil until translucent. Remove and set aside. Beat steaks (if not already tenderized) to desired consistency with a meat mallet. Salt and pepper and dredge in flour, then sear in a skillet. Remove and add broth, whisking to incorporate bits of flour stuck to the pan. If necessary, whisk in a little more flour to reach desired thickness. Return the onions to the pan, and place in oven at 400°F. In an hour to an hour and a half, check for tenderness. Serve with well-buttered mashed potatoes, topped with the gravy, with pickled beans on the side.

Rabbit Two Ways

Nate Allen

Nate's recipes are delightfully simple and effective. Most often developed on the spur of the moment with what is at hand, making the most of each ingredient in the kitchen while highlighting its specific flavor, the combination of his playfulness in not taking ingredients too seriously, and his passion for letting each ingredient sing out for itself, is what keeps his diners coming back again and again. Of course if you are rabbitophobic, you can substitute chicken wings and drumsticks, but the results will not be as savory.

For the Rabbit Wings

Front legs of several rabbits
Handful of herbs if desired
Salt and pepper to taste

Rub with salt and pepper and optional herbs. Put on sheet pan. Roast for about a half hour at 350°F.

For the Blueberry Glaze Sauce

A cup or more of blueberries
¼ cup sugar
Water to cover
1 poblano pepper
1 clove garlic
Salt and pepper to taste
Small handful of fresh basil

Boil blueberries and sugar in water. Chop and add poblano pepper, and garlic, salt, and pepper. Reduce. Throw in fresh basil. When rabbit wings are done, toss, still hot, in bowl with the glaze.

For the Rabbit Hind Legs

Hind legs of several rabbits
A tablespoon or so of oil
1 or more onion(s), depending
   on quantity of rabbit
Chicken broth to deglaze
Handful of fennel leaves
Salt and pepper to taste

Sear rabbit with oil, salt, and pepper, chop onion and place in bottom of roasting pan, lay rabbit on top, pour chicken broth around legs, lay wild fennel stem on top, cover with foil, bake 1½ hours. Remove to platter and keep warm.

For the Stem Relish
Leftover chard stems, however
    many you have
Generous fistful of parsley
Several leaves of basil
A few fennel stems or sprigs
Salt and pepper to taste

Chop all stems to nice mouth size (¼ inch or less). Toss in sauce or quick-pickle in vinegar and salt.

Author's Note: This relish can be made with any combination of leftover stems (chard, spinach, turnip greens, collards, kale, parsley...), so long as they are tender enough, and used as a garnish for meats. Alternatively, save your stems as they gather, in a freezer bag, and toss them in for flavor whenever you make a broth.

For the Chard & Kale Garnish
Briefly sauté Swiss chard and green onions or shallots with fresh garlic, salt, pepper, olive oil. Massage kale with salt. Add to sautéed chard. Throw in basil. Serve hot or cold.

For the Fresh Tomato Salad
A dozen or more cherry
    tomatoes
Several of a variety of heirloom
    tomatoes
Handful of basil leaves
Several fennel fronds
Salt and pepper to taste

Slice (halve) cherry tomatoes, wedge larger tomatoes (a variety of sizes), add salt and pepper to release juice, add basil and fennel fronds. Pour extra juice over greens for acidity.

To Serve
Confect a reduced sauce from what's left in the bottom of the pan after roasting the hind legs, throw in relish, pull rabbit apart, add to broth, serve dressed with greens and tomatoes, accompanied by the blueberry-glazed rabbit wings.

From the Stream

Where life began and life flows on

While crawdads, or crayfish, are most often associated with Louisiana, Appalachian mountain streams run rich with them as well. As a child, I spent a great deal of time wading up and down the creek and bathing in its various eddies. Many's the time I've found my toes in the vice-like grip of a crawdad. My brother and I used to boil them up for the fun of watching them turn red, although I never actually remember eating one until I traveled to New Orleans. They are excellent dipped in melted butter or tossed in a salad or thrown on top of a plate of succotash. The Crawdad Song evolved from Anglo-American play-party traditions and African-American blues.

The Crawdad Song
(Traditional)

You get a line and I'll get a pole,
   Honey,
You get a line and I'll get a pole,
   Babe.
You get a line and I'll get a pole,
We'll go fishin' in the crawdad hole,
Honey, Baby mine.

Sittin' on the bank 'til my feet get
   cold, Honey,
Sittin' on the bank 'til my feet get
   cold, Babe,
Sittin' on the bank 'til my feet get
   cold,
Lookin' down into that crawdad hole,
Honey, Baby mine.

Yonder comes a man with a sack on
   his back, Honey,
Yonder comes a man with a sack on
   his back, Babe,
Yonder comes a man with a sack on
   his back,
Packin' all the crawdads he can pack,
Honey, Baby mine.

The man fell down and he broke that
   sack, Honey,
The man fell down and he broke that
   sack, Babe,
The man fell down and he broke that
   sack,
See those crawdads backing back,
Honey, Baby mine.

What you gonna do when the lake
    goes dry, Honey,
What you gonna do when the lake
    goes dry, Babe,
What you gonna do when the lake
    goes dry,
Gonna sit on the bank and watch the
    crawdads die,
Honey, Baby mine.

What did the hen duck say to the
    drake, Honey
What did the hen duck say to the
    drake, Babe
What did the hen duck say to the
    drake
Ain't no crawdads in that lake
Honey, Baby, mine

Standin' on the corner with a dollar
    in my hand, Honey,
Standin' on the corner with a dollar
    in my hand, Babe,
Standin' on the corner with a dollar
    in my hand,
Standin' there waitin' for the craw-
    dad man,
Honey, Baby mine.

Get up, Sue, you slept too late,
    Honey,
Get up, Sue, you slept too late, Babe,
Get up, Sue, you slept too late,
That crawdad man's done passed
    your gate,
Honey, Baby mine.

*"One of life's greatest pleasures is enjoying our food
and the company of friends and family."*
—Dr. John LaPuma

Roasted Sunburst Farm Trout
Stuffed with Black Walnuts & Sunshine Squash wrapped in Napa Cabbage, served with Mark's Hard Cider Reduction

Serves 4 as luncheon, appetizer or light entrée portion

Mark Rosenstein

6 tablespoons Sunshine squash
  purée (see note below)
3 tablespoons black walnuts,
  chopped fine (by hand)
2 (6 ounce) filets Sunburst
  Farms trout, skin and pin
  bones removed
8 leaves Napa cabbage,
  blanched, drained, patted dry
1 tablespoon walnut oil
3 cups hard cider
1 teaspoon fresh thyme,
  chopped
1 tablespoon butter
Salt and pepper to taste

Equipment
Baking sheet lined with either a
  silicone baking pad or a piece
  of baking paper
Non-aluminum sauce pan

Ahead of time, make the squash purée (see notes below). Blanche, drain, and dry the Napa cabbage leaves and reserve. Preheat oven to 425°F.

Cut each filet in half. Lay four leaves of cabbage on the worktable and season with a little salt and pepper. Place 1 piece of trout on each leaf, and season with salt and pepper. Using a tablespoon, equally divide the squash purée between the filets, and spread evenly with the back of the spoon. Evenly divide the black walnuts between the filets and spread evenly on top of the squash. Place the remaining leaves of cabbage on top of the filets and fold the bottom leaves over the top. You may prepare ahead to this point.

In a non-aluminum saucepan, bring the 3 cups of hard cider to a boil, turn down the heat and cook until only 6–8 tablespoons remain. Take off the heat.

Place the filets on the baking sheet, in a preheated oven, and bake for 6–7 minutes. Serve on warmed dishes.

Return the cider to the heat, briefly. Swirl in the butter, add the chopped thyme and spoon over the top of the fish.

For the Roasted Pumpkin & Squash Filling

Select ripe pumpkins or squash without blemish. First, using a sharp, heavy knife, cut off the outer skin. Remove the stem. Cut into eighths, remove the seeds and inner membrane. Clean the seeds and reserve for toasting.

Cut the flesh roughly into 2 inch cubes. In a bowl ample enough to hold all the flesh, season with salt, pepper, oil (just enough to coat the flesh), and any spice (sweet spice, curry spice, etc.).

In a moderately slow oven, roast the flesh until tender. Allow to cool and then purée. This is a basic preparation. It may be refrigerated for a week, frozen or canned.

This preparation is one of my "Paint Pots," that is, it is something in my basic cooking palette, especially for fall and early winter. Here are other ways to use it:

- Combine the purée with some chicken or vegetable stock for a soup.

- Make a ravioli, either with fresh pasta or using wanton wrappers. Variation: add a cheese, such as feta, a blue, or other favorite.

- Make a vegetable mousse/timbale: Combine with a few eggs, a bit of cream and fill a small mold. Bake in bain marie until set.

- Confect a soufflé, either savory or sweet.

A Note about Winter Squashes: Ubiquitous in the garden, there are more than 150 varieties of the hard-skinned winter variety of squashes. Few make their presence known in the kitchen, which is a shame, as there are few vegetables that when properly cooked blend such an inherently creamy texture with such an earthy and often sweet flavor. The color of the flavor is reflected in the color of the flesh—deep rust, a rich and lingering earthy taste that haunts the palate, especially when highlighted by a curry spice or one based on cloves. Bright orange: zesty and sweet, when blended with citrus zest and butter it makes a wonderful base for simmering mild fleshed birds such as turkey or chicken.

Mountain Trout Stuffed with Ramps   Serves 4

Mark Rosenstein

4 whole, small, fresh trout, de-boned (rib cage and back bone removed)

2 tablespoons bacon fat or olive oil

1 good handful of fresh ramps, cleaned, cut into 1-inch pieces (reserve some of the green tops for cooking with potatoes)

4 handfuls of dandelion greens, cleaned, stems removed

2 cups cooked corn grits, fairly soft

2 more tablespoons rendered bacon fat or olive oil

Knob of butter

Dash of vinegar

Salt and pepper to taste

De-bone the trout, leaving whole. Season the cavity with salt and pepper. In a heavy iron skillet (select a skillet large enough to hold all four trout), heat the first 2 tablespoons of fat over medium heat. Cook the ramps until lightly browned. Add the dandelion greens and cook until they are wilted and all the water evaporates. Season with salt and pepper. Add the soft corn grits to the mixture, mix well, and heat through. Remove from heat.

Divide the mixture into four parts and stuff the trout. Reshape the fish. Wipe out the skillet. Over medium flame, heat the remaining 2 tablespoons of fat. Add the trout and cook on the first side, about 4 minutes, until the skin is crispy. Turn over and cook on the second side until brown and crispy. Place the trout on four heated dinner plates. Wipe out the iron skillet, add a healthy knob of butter. Cook until the butter just begins to brown. Add a dash of vinegar (or lemon juice) and pour over the fish.

Serve with some very crispy hash browns, seasoned with the green tops of the ramps, cut in ribbons.

Cornmeal-Crusted Trout with Hominy Hoppin' John
& Pickled Blueberry Mostarda

Bradley Griffin

Chef Griffin kindly shared this recipe of his from the Harvest Table Restaurant in Meadowview, Virginia, which began as an extension of the bestselling book Animal, Vegetable, Miracle, written by celebrated author Barbara Kingsolver, her husband, Harvest Table Director Steven Hopp, and their two daughters. The story, about one family's yearlong experiment to eat only in-season locally grown foods (no bananas!), has become far more than just their story. When I first encountered this work, I thought, "What's the fuss about? This is exactly how I ate when I was growing up!" And then it quickly became apparent that the principles were novel thinking to a large part of America, and people were hungry for just this kind of inspiration to give them a new sense of direction in their own culinary quests. Barbara and her family dared to share it with the world, and the world has been a better place ever since.

For the Trout
1 trout per person
Self-rising cornmeal, to dredge
Salt and pepper to taste
Oil for pan

Mix cornmeal, salt, and pepper. Dredge trout through cornmeal mixture. Place in a hot, oiled sauté pan and cook, flesh side down, until golden brown. Flip and cook until skin is crisp.

For the Hoppin' John
½ cup country ham, diced
2 cups cooked hominy
1½ cups almost cooked rice
3 cups water

Cook ham in a large sauté pan. Add hominy and rice. Add water to pan and lower heat to medium-low. Simmer until most of the liquid is evaporated.

For the Pickled Blueberries
2 cups fresh blueberries
3 cups lemon juice
1 cup red wine vinegar
1 sprig rosemary
2 tablespoons fennel seeds

In a medium saucepan, combine vinegar, sugar, lemon juice, rosemary, and fennel. Bring to a boil. Pour liquid over blueberries and place in refrigerator for 15–20 minutes.

For the Mostarda
1 cup pickled blueberries
2 cups pickle liquid
1 teaspoon mustard powder
1 teaspoon Dijon mustard

In a small sauce pot, add blueberries, pickle liquid, mustard powder, and Dijon mustard. Cook on medium-high until liquid evaporates and sauce has a jam-like consistency, approximately 20 minutes.

To Plate
Place a dollop of rice (prepare as preferred) on the center of a plate. Spoon on a portion of the Hoppin' John, layer the crusted trout on top of your base, add a generous spoonful of the pickled mostarda, and top with microgreens.

"One of the delights of life is eating with friends, second to that is talking about eating. And, for an unsurpassed double whammy, there is talking about eating while you are eating with friends."
—LAURIE COLWIN

Cast Iron Trout, Smoked Grits, Farm Egg, & Potlikker Jus `Serves 12`

William Dissen

This dish is designed for a generous number of guests. Halve it if cooking for six, or quarter it if cooking for three. Or reserve it for that occasion when Aunt Judy and Uncle Slim drop in with a following of children and you really don't know how you will feed all those mouths. Eggs and grits are usually always on hand (at least in an Appalachian household), and trout should not be hard to come by. At the very least you can send all the men out to the nearest sporting goods store to pick up a fishing pole and license, and profit from a few hours of peace before they return!

For the Grits
4 tablespoons blended olive oil
½ cup red onion, small dice
2 tablespoons garlic, minced
4 cups yellow corn grits, coarse ground
16 cups water
3 cups heavy cream
1 cup chèvre* (unaged goat cheese)
4 tablespoons Frank's Red Hot Sauce
Salt and pepper to taste

For the Farm Eggs
16 farm eggs
Salt and pepper to taste

For the Potlikker Jus
3 quarts potlikker jus**
2 tablespoons butter
Salt and pepper to taste

For the Trout
3 tablespoons blended oil
6 trout, pin bones out
Salt and pepper to taste

For the Garnish
36 pickled ramps, cut lengthwise on the bias
¼ cup parsley, finely chopped
Aleppo pepper, as needed

Author's Note: Chèvre as an ingredient has always irked me. "Chèvre" in French, from which the term was taken, means goat. So when someone puts chèvre on the menu, it means literally that he is serving goat. The best term for this particular ingredient should be, if kept in French, "fromage de chèvre," Otherwise, the best term in English is "goat cheese," or "unaged goat cheese," which it has somehow come to mean by assumption.

**"Jus" means juice in French. Here we are talking about the juice left at the bottom of a pot when the main ingredient has been served.*

For the Grits

Place the grits a half-inch layer on a hotel pan. Place in a smoker and smoke for 45 minutes. Allow to cool. In a medium pot, heat the oil over medium-high heat and add the onion. Cook until translucent and stir in the garlic. Cook for another 30 seconds and pour in the water. Bring the water to a boil over high heat. As the water comes to a boil, whisk in the grits, constantly stirring until they come together and begin to bubble, about 3–4 minutes. As the grits begin to bubble, remove the pot from the heat and immediately cover with plastic wrap and aluminum foil, and keep in a warm place. Allow to steam for 45–50 minutes. After the grits have steamed, place the pot back on stove over medium heat. Stir in the heavy cream, chèvre, Frank's Red Hot, salt, and pepper, and bring to a simmer. Taste and re-season as necessary. Serve immediately, if possible.

For the Farm Eggs

Bring an immersion circulator in a water bath to 64°C (147°F). Position the eggs in a pasta basket and place in the water bath. Allow to cook for 50 minutes.

For the Potlikker Jus

Bring the potlikker jus to a simmer and mount in the butter, incorporating a little at a time, by whisking. Season to taste with salt and pepper.

For the Trout

Cut the trout filets into 2 portions each, discarding the tail end. Season the skin side of the trout with salt and pepper. In a large cast iron pan, heat the oil over medium-high heat and as the oil begins to shimmer, place the trout into the pan (skin side down), and allow to cook until the trout skin is crispy. Gently turn the trout over and reduce the heat to medium. Allow to cook for another 3–4 minutes, or until the trout is cooked through.

To Serve

Place a small cast iron serving skillet over a folded napkin on a small square plate. Place a 3-inch ring mold into the center of the round skillet. Place a teaspoon of the grits in the center of the ring mold. Crack a poached egg into a perforated bar straining spoon and place the egg directly on the grits. Gently mound more of the grits over the poached egg. Then place a piece of trout (skin side up) on the grits. Pour approximately 2 ounces of potlikker jus around the outside of the ring mold and garnish the trout with the sliced, pickled ramps. Garnish the plate with the chopped parsley and Aleppo pepper.

Pan-Seared Filet of Trout with Black Walnut Flour `Serves 4`

Mark Rosenstein

For the Filets

4 trout filets, each weighing 5
ounces
1 cup seasoned black walnut flour
A few tablespoons clarified butter
for sauté and dredging
2 tablespoons chopped parsley
1 tablespoon fresh marjoram
½ ounce Jack Daniels
6 ounces cider fish fumet

For the Walnut Flour

¾ cup black walnuts*
¼ cup all-purpose flour
Salt and pepper to taste

*You may substitute English
walnuts, but the dish is not
as robust.*

In slow oven, roast ¾ cup walnuts until light brown. Allow to cool. In food processor, using pulse technique, chop the walnuts with ¼ cup all-purpose flour seasoned with salt and pepper, until a coarse meal is achieved.

For the Cider-Fish Fumet

Several fish bones
White wine and water to cover
Juice of one lemon Mushroom
trimmings
Handful of fresh or dried herbs
Salt and pepper to taste
2 tablespoons cider reduction

To 1 cup fish fumet (the liquid from fish bones boiled down with white wine, water, lemon juice, mushroom trimmings, herbs, and spices), add 2 tablespoons of cider reduction (cider boiled down until it is concentrate). Reduce by 20% more.

For the Filets

Dip trout filets in melted clarified butter, let excess liquid drip off, dredge the filets on both sides in the meal. Press meal into filet to help stick. Sauté trout in a heavy skillet over medium heat, using clarified butter, 3 to 4 minutes on a side, until light golden color. Remove to a warm dish or serving plate. Wipe excess meal from skillet, deglaze with Jack Daniels, add fish fumet, parsley, and marjoram, and pour over fish. Serve immediately, with pan-roasted potatoes and onions and winter greens.

"Cooking is a language through which all the following properties may be expressed: harmony, creativity, happiness, beauty, poetry, complexity, magic, humour, provocation and culture."
—FERRAN ADRIA

Oat-Crusted Trout
with Red Sauce Vinaigrette & Carolina Slaw
Paul Rankin & Nick Nairn

This is a wild-card recipe in that it comes not from an Appalachian chef per se, but from a pair of Michelin-starred Irish and Scottish chefs, featured on a program known as Paul & Nick's Big American Food Trip, which is produced by Waddell Media of County Down, Ireland. In the summer of 2015, top chefs and great friends Paul Rankin and Nick Nairn journeyed across the sea to the States, to follow the trail of the first Ulster-Scots who settled in the New World. During their visits to Virginia, North and South Carolina, and East Tennessee, they stopped in Madison County, North Carolina, where they fished from the Shelton Laurel River and prepared a dinner fit for kings in my own modest kitchen, serving it up for friends and family of Scots-Irish heritage in front of my cabin porch overlooking the mountains which separate North Carolina from Tennessee, the Appalachian Trail marking the border. The following recipes are their tribute to their people who carried in times of hardship not only their culinary touch but their music and their dance to these mountains, which gave them a second chance at life.

For the Trout

4 trout, scaled, fileted, pin bones
   removed
200 grams (1 cup) rolled oats
1 tablespoon Cajun spice (salt,
   pepper, cayenne, garlic)
2 tablespoons olive oil

Scale, filet, and remove the pin bones from each trout. Carefully remove the skin and set aside. Coat the trout filets in rolled oats (made more fine by a moment in the blender) and Cajun spice.

Lay the skin on a flat baking tray, brush with oil, and place in the oven at 180°C (350°F) for 10 minutes or until crispy.

Heat a large frying pan and add oil. Place the oat-crusted trout filets skin side down, and pan fry until the filets begin to turn golden. Flip the filets over and continue cooking for 3–4 minutes longer until cooked through.

Remove the crispy skin from the oven and set aside.

For the Red Sauce Vinaigrette

1 tablespoon tomato ketchup
1 tablespoon hot sauce
2 tablespoons olive oil
2 tablespoons water
1 teaspoon Cajun spice
1 tablespoon spring onions,
    chopped
Salt and pepper to taste

To make the red sauce, mix together in a large bowl the ketchup and hot sauce. Next, slowly add the oil until combined. If the sauce is looking too thick, loosen with a splash of water.

To finish the sauce, add the spring onions and season with Cajun spice. Check seasoning, and add salt and pepper if needed.

For the Carolina Slaw

1 cabbage
1 bunch radishes
2 kohlrabi
3 carrots
1 bunch coriander
4 spring onions
1 green chili

Finely shred all the slaw ingredients on a mandolin. Mix well in a large bowl and add the dressing.

Carolina Slaw Dressing

1 tablespoon peanut butter
2 tablespoons lime juice
1 teaspoon sugar
1 teaspoon Carolina hot sauce
1 teaspoon Cajun seasoning
1 tablespoon water

Place the peanut butter in a bowl with a splash of water, mix well to loosen the peanut butter, and add the lime juice and hot sauce. Next, add the sugar to balance the heat, and then pour over the shredded slaw ingredients. Mix well.

To Serve

Place the Carolina slaw just off center on the plate, with the trout filet to one side. Next, drizzle the red sauce around the plate and place the crispy skin up against the filet.

The Backbone

Main courses to satisfy the soul

According to a Kentucky Historical Society roadway sign, Old Joe Clark is a mountain ballad about 90 stanzas long, sung during World War I and later by soldiers from eastern Kentucky. An early version, as sung in Virginia, was printed in 1918. Joe Clark, born in 1839, was regarded as a shiftless and rough mountaineer. In the moonshining days of the 1870s, he ran a government-supervised still. He was murdered in 1885. The following selection of verses are favorites from my father's repertoire.

Old Joe Clark

(Traditional)

I went down to Old Joe Clark's
I'd never been there before
He fed me out of a hog trough
And I won't go there no more

Old Joe Clark had an old red house
Sixteen stories high
And every story in that house
Was filled with chicken pie

Old Joe Clark was a preacher
His church was always full
The neighbors came from miles
   around
To hear him shoot the bull

I went down to old Joe's house
Old Joe wasn't home
I ate up all of old Joe's meat
And fed the dog the bone

I took my wife to Old Joe's house
He invited us to supper
She stumped her toe on the table leg
And stuck her nose in the butter

When Old Joe Clark comes to my
   door
He treats me like a pup
He runs my bear dogs under the floor
And drinks my whiskey up

He puts his banjer in my hand
And tells me what to play
And dances with my pretty little girl
Until the break of day

I wouldn't marry Old Joe Clark
I'll tell you the reason why
He's always chawin' tobaccer
And his chin is never dry

Old Joe Clark he had a dog
As blind as he could be
Chased a redbug 'round a stump
And a coon up a hollow tree

Old Joe had a yellow cat
Would neither sing nor pray
She stuck her head in a buttermilk
   jar
And washed her sins away

Old Joe Clark has an old red cow
I know her by the bell

If she ever gets in my cornfield
I'll shoot her sure as...

Old Joe Clark's a fine old man
Tell you the reason why
He keeps good likker 'round his
   house
It's good old Rock and Rye

Fare thee well, Old Joe Clark
Fare thee well, I'm gone
Fare thee well, Old Joe Clark
I feel like trav'lin' on

Ralph's Chicken and Dumplings

Ralph Lewis

The following recipe was garnered over the space of an hour while chowing down on steak and wings in a chain establishment in Canton, North Carolina. Ralph's daughter Sherry adds her reflections at the end. Other siblings (Welynn, Marty, Don) have different memories as well. I'll leave it to you, the reader, to decide which angle to develop. Be sure to don your cap of choice and proclaim unabashedly with 88-year-old Ralph, "I'm the chef of the world...Whoo!"

2 whole chickens, cut into pieces
Shortening (lard, butter or
   Crisco) for both frying and
   confecting dumpling batter
Flour for dumplings, about 2
   cups
Milk for dumplings, about 1 cup
Salt and pepper to taste
(Beer, for drinking while
   cooking)

Salt and pepper and sear chicken pieces in a skillet in Crisco, until just brown but not dark (the sound you want here is "pshhh"). Transfer to large pot with lid and add water to cover. Simmer for an hour or until tender, making sure the liquid goes "bli-lip...bli-lip...bli...lip..." (This is the sound large, slow bubbles make, for anyone who relies on auditory signals in the kitchen!)

Meanwhile, pour a beer to drink while you wait, and confect dumplings with flour, in the middle of which you make a well and add milk and shortening. When it is the right consistency (not too dry, not too wet), pinch off little bits and roll small balls (about shooter marble size) and coat with flour.

Heat shortening in another skillet and deep fry dumplings until golden. Add dumplings to pot, serve it up and...Whoo! Lordy!

Note from Ralph's daughter, Sherry Lewis Morgan

He only stewed the chicken, no frying. We made the dumplings the same way we make homemade biscuits: milk, Crisco, and self-rising flour. No measurements, not too wet and not too dry, so he got that right, but he just spooned the dumplings in without coating them with flour, about the size of a teaspoon. He used a table knife. He took the stewed meat out of the pot and added about a half stick of butter to the broth and seasoned it with salt and pepper to taste. You need at least half of your largest pot filled with broth and bring it to a rolling boil before you start dropping dumplings. Use the back of a large spoon to push the dumplings under and slowly stir the bottom of the pot to keep them from scorching. Lower the heat and keep pushing the dumplings down until you test a few to make sure the dumplings are done. Skin the meat and remove it off the bone by pinching it into pieces, and add it back to the pot. The dumplings were never fried.

Ralph's Surprise Supper

Ralph Lewis

The beauty of this simple recipe is that it can be made, typical Appalachian style, from almost nothing, and can serve the dual purpose of cleaning out your refrigerator and feeding your family something delicious in very little time. Fancy recipes are wonderful, but feeding a family or even yourself every single day is the biggest challenge. This will help make the task easier.

Meat of any kind that needs
   using up
Lawry's Seasoning*

*Lawry's Seasoning was created by Lawry Frank around 1922, and was the first seasoned salt to hit the market. Later purchased and marketed by McCormick, it is a blend of salt, sugar, and spices, including paprika, turmeric, onion, and garlic.

Put chunks of any kind of meat, tossed in Lawry's Seasoning, on a sheet of foil, close together, in baking dish. Bake at 350°F for 25 minutes, then check for tenderness. Serve with mashed potatoes and sweet pickles and cornbread.

"Sharing food with another human being is an intimate act that should not be indulged in lightly."
—M.F.K. FISHER

Pan-Roasted Duck Breast
with Braised Greens, Cider-Sautéed Mushrooms & Spinach Gastrique

Bradley Griffin

For the Duck
Duck breasts, 1 per 2–3 people
Salt and pepper to taste

With a sharp knife, score the duck, going ¼ into the fat side. Rotate 90° and repeat. Season with salt and pepper. Place the duck breast fat side down in a cold, lightly oiled pan. Turn the heat to high and sear the duck breast on all sides. Place the pan in an oven at 350°F for 5 minutes or until done. Allow duck to rest 5 minutes before slicing.

For the Braised Greens

1 pound mizuna or other
  hearty green
2 cups vegetable stock
2 cups red wine vinegar
1 tablespoon cloves, whole
2 tablespoons fennel seeds

Bring vinegar, cloves, fennel seeds, and stock to a boil. Add the mizuna, reduce heat to medium-low, and simmer 20 minutes.

For the Cider-Sautéed Mushrooms

1 pound shiitake mushrooms
1 cup hard apple cider
  (I suggest Foggy Ridge
  Pippin Black)
Salt and pepper to taste

Slice the mushrooms. Place them in a hot, unoiled pan. Season with salt and pepper. Cook mushrooms 5 minutes. Deglaze with the hard apple cider and reduce until all liquid evaporates.

For the Spinach Gastrique

½ pound spinach
2 cups lemon juice
2 cups sugar

Combine the sugar and lemon juice in a saucepan and cook on high for 10 minutes or until the sugar has caramelized. Add the spinach, and stir until the spinach is wilted. Purée and allow to cool.

To Plate

Arrange braised greens around half of outside edge of plate. Dot with mushrooms. Slice duck breast ½ inch thick and arrange, overlapping, inside the semi-circle of greens. Drizzle with the Spinach Gastrique.

Grilled Halibut with Herb- & Garlic-Roasted New Potatoes
& Summer Tomato & Orange Relish   Serves 4

James Boyce

6–8 small red potatoes (about 1½ pounds)
1 head garlic, papery outer skin removed
1 sprig rosemary
1 sprig thyme
⅓ cup olive oil

4 medium vine-ripe tomatoes (red or yellow)
¼ cup sherry vinegar
2 tablespoons freshly squeezed orange juice
4 halibut or sea bass filets
Salt and pepper to taste

Preheat an outdoor grill to medium-high. Scrub the potatoes, pat dry, cut into quarters, and put in a medium bowl. Cut the head of garlic into 4 pieces and add to the bowl with the sprigs of rosemary and thyme. Toss with 2 tablespoons of the olive oil, and season with salt and pepper. Empty the contents of the bowl onto a large sheet of aluminum foil, then fold the sides up to enclose the potatoes in a pouch. Set the pouch on the hot grill, and roast until the potatoes are tender, 15–20 minutes. Move the package to the outer edge of the grill to keep warm.

While the potatoes are roasting, bring a small pan half-filled with water to a boil. Core the tomatoes and cut a small "X" on the bottom of each tomato. Gently add them to the boiling water and simmer until the tomato skin begins to split, about 30 seconds. Immediately transfer the tomatoes to a bowl of ice water and let the tomatoes cool. Drain the tomatoes, cut them in half, and scoop out and discard the seeds. Dice the tomatoes and combine them with the remaining olive oil, vinegar, and orange juice. Season to taste with salt and pepper, toss to mix well, and set aside.

Season the halibut with salt and pepper, and cook on the grill until the fish is just opaque through, about 5 to 7 minutes on each side, depending on the thickness of the fish.

Arrange the roasted potatoes in a small pile on each plate, set the fish on top, and spoon the tomato relish around the filet. Garnish with orange segments and a sprig of fresh basil.

Bourbon-Marinated Flank Steak with Blueberry Barbecue Sauce

Mary Collins-Shepard

For the Steak

(Marinate at least 2 hours or overnight)

2 flank steaks, each about 1½ pounds

½ cup bourbon

¼ cup soy sauce

¼ cup olive oil

¼ cup local honey

For the Sauce

Makes about 1½ cups

2 cups blueberries

⅓ cup honey

Juice and grated zest from 1 orange

1 tablespoon ketchup

1 teaspoon chili powder

1 teaspoon balsamic vinegar

2 tablespoons bourbon (optional)

2 tablespoons cold unsalted butter

¼ teaspoon each sea salt and freshly ground pepper, or to taste

For the Steak

Prepare a gas or charcoal (preferred) grill for high heat grilling. Remove steak from marinade, let excess liquid drip off, and place on the grill. For medium rare, cook 4–5 minutes per side or to an internal temperature of 145°F. Brush with barbecue sauce during the last minute of cooking. Remove from the grill to a carving board; cover loosely with foil and let rest 10 minutes.

To serve, slice steak thinly, against the grain and serve with extra sauce at table.

For the Sauce

Purée blueberries in a blender. Place purée in a small, non-reactive saucepan; add honey, orange juice and zest, ketchup, chili powder, and vinegar. Bring to a simmer, stirring occasionally. Simmer, uncovered, 2 minutes. Remove from heat, and whisk in butter and salt and pepper. Taste and adjust seasoning. Store leftovers in a covered container in refrigerator for up to 1 week.

Black-Eyed Pea, Collard, & Sweet Potato Stew

Denny Trantham

This is a hearty vegetable dish to serve as a main course when you feel like going meatless. It can also be served as a side to any of the heftier meat dishes found earlier in this book.

1 pound fresh collard greens
1 medium-sized yellow onion, halved
6 whole cloves
2 tablespoons bacon grease
3 bay leaves
1 fresh garlic bulb, peeled and diced
1 teaspoon dried crushed red pepper
1 tablespoon dried mustard
4 tablespoons brown sugar
½ cup cider vinegar
2 smoked ham hocks
1 pound pork neck bones
1 (16-ounce) package dried black-eyed peas
2 medium-sized sweet potatoes, peeled and cubed
6 cups hot cooked rice
¼ cup coarsely chopped parsley leaves
¼ cup coarsely chopped cilantro leaves
2 teaspoons kosher salt
Freshly ground black pepper to taste
Hot sauce to taste

Chop collard leaves after removing stems. Insert 3 whole cloves in each onion half, and place onions and hot bacon grease in a Dutch oven over medium-high heat. Add next 10 ingredients. Add 4 quarts water, simmering and stirring gently for 3 hours, or until ham hocks are tender and potlikker is rich in flavor.

Add drained peas, and simmer for an additional 20 minutes. Stir in sweet potatoes, and cook, stirring occasionally, 10 minutes or until peas and sweet potatoes are both tender. Stir in 2 teaspoons kosher salt. Add freshly ground black pepper and hot sauce to taste. Adjust seasoning if desired. Serve stew over hot cooked rice, and sprinkle with chopped fresh flat-leaf parsley and chopped fresh cilantro. Serve with hot sauce on the side.

Chicken Breasts with Sweet Onion & Tomato Ragoût   Serves 4

Denny Trantham

4 skin-on chicken breasts,
   sautéed golden brown
⅛–¼ pound pancetta, cut into
   small pieces (or 2 slices bacon,
   bacon grease, or olive oil)
½ pound sweet onions,
   julienned
¼ pound local grape tomatoes,
   split
2 tablespoons fresh chives, diced
3 tablespoons good sherry
   vinegar
1 tablespoon local sorghum
   molasses
¼ cup heavy cream
Salt and pepper to taste

For Ragoût
In a large skillet, cook pancetta until it begins to curl. Add sweet onions as they're prepped, stirring to coat with fat and then occasionally, until they're nearly cooked. Stir in the vinegar and let cook down until almost gone. Stir in the cream and cook down until almost absorbed. Finish by folding in the tomatoes, chives, and molasses at the very end, adjusting seasoning as necessary.

To Plate
Top chicken breasts with Ragoût, and serve with collard greens and smashed potatoes.

Southern-Style Sweet Tea-Brined Fried Chicken

Denny Trantham

A classic Sunday-after-church or church supper favorite, fried chicken is practically a religion unto itself. Denny takes this recipe to new heights with his sweet tea brine and his sweet onion gravy.

For the Sweet Tea-Brined Fried Chicken
4 (6-ounce) boneless chicken breasts

For the Brine
1 quart sweet tea
1 quart unsweet tea
1 whole lemon, halved
4 bay leaves, rubbed
2 teaspoons whole peppercorns
2 tablespoons salt
Pinch dried thyme, or one fresh stem

For the Egg Wash
2 large eggs
2 tablespoons milk
1½ teaspoons Worcestershire sauce
1 tablespoon black pepper
2 teaspoons kosher salt
A few dashes Crystal hot sauce

For the Dry Rub
2 pounds all-purpose flour
1 tablespoon garlic powder
1 tablespoon onion powder
1½ teaspoons parsley flakes
1 teaspoon cayenne pepper
1 tablespoon black pepper
2 teaspoons kosher salt

For the Sweet Onion Gravy
2 cups flour
1¾ cups vegetable or canola oil
2 cups chicken stock
1 cup sweet tea
1 cup unsweet tea
1 Vidalia onion, or yellow onion, cut into semi circles

Place whole, thawed, boneless chicken breasts into brine. Store in refrigerator overnight, or for a minimum of one hour. Remove chicken from the container, taking out all seasoning pieces, and pat dry with paper towel or clean kitchen towel. Place the chicken in egg wash, then into flour.

Deep fry in oil at 350°F for 5 to 7 minutes until golden brown, or until the internal temperature of the chicken reaches 165°F for 15 seconds. Set aside.

Season to taste with garlic and onion powders, black pepper, and kosher salt. Add oil to 2-quart sauce pan, heat on medium-high, incorporate flour with whisk. Continue to stir until homogenous. Into the blonde roux, pour the chicken stock and the tea. Whisk until smooth, thinning with water as needed. Gravy should coat the back of a spoon. Once smooth, add onions to gravy. Cook until onions are tender, reducing the gravy. Plate the chicken and top with gravy…BOOM!!!

Tea-Smoked Quail Breast Serves 8

John Fleer

16 quail breasts

For the Apple Cider Brine
1 quart apple cider
1 shallot, minced
2 cloves garlic, sliced
½ teaspoon black pepper
¼ cup soy sauce
2 tablespoons brown sugar
¼ cup kosher salt
1 clove star anise
¼ cup apple cider vinegar
3 cups ice water

For the Tea Smoke
6 cups sugar
2 large black tea bags (Lipton)
2 star anise

For the Apple Cider Brine
Bring cider, onions, garlic, pepper, soy sauce, sugar, salt, anise, and vinegar to a boil. Remove from heat and add ice water. Stir and cool thoroughly before use. Submerge quail breasts in brine for 3 hours. Remove from brine and let air dry for 2 hours in refrigerator.

For the Tea Smoke
To smoke quail, line a roasting pan with aluminum foil. Pour sugar into roasting pan and set over medium flame until sugar begins to caramelize and smoke. Pour tea leaves over burning sugar. Set quail over roasting pan in a perforated pan. Invert another roasting pan on top of quail to create a stovetop smoker. Let smoke for 6–8 minutes until outside of quail is tea-smoked color but still rare. Finish cooking to desired temperature in the oven.

Braised Pork Belly with Savoy Cabbage & Black Walnuts

Serves 8 as appetizer or luncheon course

Mark Rosenstein

When I was a child, one of my most poignant taste memories surrounded the yearly ritual of hog-killing. While the action that brought the hog from his pen to the table was what held my fascination the most, the ensuing repast around the neighbor's table was just as appealing.

Plates of cornbread, biscuits, white bread, sliced tomatoes, bowls of soupbeans, turnip greens, sausage balls, corn on the cob were passed around, along with pitchers of sweet tea, coffee, fresh spring water. Homemade pickles, relish, apple butter, battered and deep-fried okra...I drank it all in, captivated by the mounds of food, transported by the savory sausage, left over from last year's hog but no less wonderful.

Beyond grace, no one spoke much except to say, "Pass the salt," but there was harmony of folks who had worked together for a common purpose. And in the satisfaction of a job well done, nothing could be more natural than sitting down together to the fruits of their labor.
—SG Séguret

1 pound pork belly
1 tablespoon salt
1 peeled carrot, cut to bite size
1 rib celery, cut to bite size
2 ribs fennel, cut to bite size
1 medium onion, peeled and
   sliced
2 cloves chopped garlic
2 tablespoons black walnut
   vinegar
1 tablespoon sourwood honey
1 cup chicken stock (plus water
   to cover)
3 sprigs fresh thyme
1 sprig fresh rosemary
Fresh ground black pepper to
   taste

For the Savoy Cabbage

1 small head of cabbage
   cut into chiffonade
A few tablespoons of the
   rendered pork fat
¼ cup black walnuts
Salt and pepper to taste

Score the pork and salt, leaving to set for 2 hours. Over medium-low heat in a heavy casserole, brown the pork on both sides. Fat will render. When pork is browned, remove. Add carrot, celery, onion, fennel, and garlic. Cook for about 5 minutes, just until they take on some color.

Drain off all the fat (reserve for cooking). Return the pork to the casserole. Deglaze the pot with the vinegar, add the honey and chicken stock. Add some water, if there is not enough liquid to cover the meat. Bring liquid to a simmer, put lid on, and put in 250°F oven. Cook for about 2½ hours, until meat is very tender. Remove from oven, place pork on a plate, strain out the vegetables, reserving for later. Pour the cooking liquid through a strainer and allow the fat to settle to the top. Either spoon off the fat, or siphon the cooking liquid to separate the two. Reserve the cooking liquid for later.

To finish the pork, cut the belly into 8 equal portions. In a heavy skillet over medium heat, brown the pork on both sides. Keep warm while cooking the cabbage.

For the Savoy Cabbage

In a large heavy sauté pan, over medium heat, cook the cabbage in the pork fat. Season with salt and pepper to taste. Cook about 5 minutes, until tender. Add the reserved vegetables from the braising, heat through, add the black walnuts. Deglaze the pan with some of the reserved cooking liquid. Portion the cabbage/vegetables onto 8 warm plates, place the finished pork belly on top, and pour the remaining cooking liquid over the top. Serve.

Braised Lamb Shanks with Chestnuts

Mark Rosenstein

8 lamb shanks

Salt and pepper, generous
  quantity

Medici spice (see page 124)

1–2 onions, diced

A few branches of celery, diced

A few carrots, diced

A few tablespoons flour

A few sprigs thyme

A few sprigs parsley

1 bay leaf

1 pound chestnuts

Red wine, to cover

Season the lamb shanks with salt and pepper, then rub with the spice and let cure for 6 hours.

In a heavy casserole, over medium-low heat, brown the shanks in the oil. Remove and set aside. Brown the diced onion, celery, and carrot in the casserole, adding additional oil if necessary. Sprinkle with flour and cook for 3 minutes. Return the lamb shanks to the casserole, add the thyme, parsley and bay leaf. Pour the red wine over the meat, bring to a simmer, and cover. Place in a slow oven (~350°F) and braise until tender.

Remove the shanks, pull the meat off the bones, discarding any tough pieces of the tendons. Place the meat into a pre-warmed serving dish. Discard the bones. Strain the cooking liquid. Return the liquid to the casserole, add the chestnuts, and simmer 5 minutes, until the chestnuts are tender. Spoon the sauce over the meat and serve, garnished with the chestnuts. Accompany with mashed parsnips and potatoes.

Medici Compilation Spice Mixture

1 tablespoon lemon zest
1½ tablespoons cinnamon
2 tablespoon coriander

1 tablespoon nutmeg
2 teaspoons cloves

Combine and grind in a spice grinder.

Benton's Bacon Fat-Seared Beef Striploin
with Barbequed Sweetbreads & Hakurei Turnips

Serves 12

William Dissen

For the Barbequed Sweetbreads
2 pounds veal sweetbreads
½ gallon milk (to soak sweetbreads)
1 pint Wondra Flour* to taste
1 gallon vegetable oil (to deep fry)
Salt and pepper to taste

For the Barbeque Sauce
1 tablespoon butter
1 yellow onion, small dice
2 tablespoons garlic, minced
20 ounces ketchup
1 cup water
14 ounces crushed tomatoes, canned
1 cup white distilled vinegar
¼ cup light brown sugar
2 tablespoons sorghum
2 tablespoons grain mustard
Salt and pepper to taste
1 tablespoon hickory smoke powder, or to taste

For the Purée
2½ quarts Hakurei** turnip bulbs, quartered
2 quarts heavy cream
1 tablespoon butter
Salt and pepper to taste

For the Sauté
2 tablespoons blended olive oil
2 pounds Hakurei turnip greens, large chiffonade
¼ cup shallot, minced
2 tablespoons garlic, minced
½ teaspoon red pepper flakes
2 tablespoons chicken stock
1 tablespoon butter
Salt and pepper to taste

For the Striploin
4 pounds beef striploin, trimmed and portioned
1 pound Benton's Bacon
Sea salt as needed
Black pepper as needed

For the Garnish
24 micro radish sprouts

For the Turnip Bulbs

Place the quartered turnip bulbs in a medium pot and cover with the heavy cream. Bring to a simmer over medium heat and cook until tender, about 15–20 minutes. Strain the turnips, reserving the cooking liquid. Place the turnips in a blender and add back 1 cup of the cooking liquid, the butter, and salt and pepper. Purée until smooth, then pass the turnip purée through the strainer into a small pot to remove any lumps. Cover the pot and keep warm.

For the Turnip Greens

In a large sauté pan, add the oil, shallot, garlic, and red pepper flakes, and cook over medium-high heat until translucent, about 1 minute. Add the turnip greens, butter, and the stock. Season with salt and pepper. Cook quickly to barely wilt the greens. Serve immediately.

For the Barbeque Sauce

In a medium sauce pan, heat the butter over medium heat and add the onions. Cook until translucent and stir in the garlic until aromatic. Add the ketchup, water, crushed tomatoes, white vinegar, brown sugar, sorghum, and grain mustard. Bring to a simmer and allow to cook for 15 minutes. Purée the barbeque sauce and finish with salt and pepper, hickory smoke powder, and butter.

For the Sweetbreads

In advance, remove any connective tissue from the sweetbreads, place in a container and cover with milk.

Allow to sit under refrigeration overnight. Then drain, rinse, and dry the sweetbreads. Bring a pot of stock to a simmer and prepare an ice bath. Place the sweetbreads in the simmering stock for 2–3 minutes. Using a slotted spoon, transfer the sweetbreads to an ice bath to immediately cool. Once cool, transfer to a towel to dry. Bring a medium pot of vegetable oil to 375°F. Portion the sweetbreads into small, bite-sized nuggets (about 1–2 inches square). In a medium bowl, toss the sweetbread nuggets in seasoned Wondra flour, shaking off any excess. Place the sweetbreads into the oil to deep fry. Cook until golden brown. Using a slotted spoon, transfer the sweetbreads to a towel to drain, and season with salt and pepper. Immediately place the sweetbreads in a medium bowl and add the barbeque sauce to coat. Serve immediately.

For the Striploin

Grind the Benton's Bacon through a medium dye. Place in a small pot and render out the fat over low heat, about 30 minutes. Strain the fat and reserve. Butcher the striploin into four 1-pound rectangular portions (approximately 2 inches x 2 inches x 8 inches). Season with fleur de sel*** and black pepper. Heat a large cast iron pan over medium-high heat and add the bacon fat. As the fat begins to shimmer, place the steak into the pan and cook until medium rare. Allow to rest for 5 minutes, slice, and season with more fleur de sel.

To Plate

Smear a long strip of turnip purée along the edge of a wood cutting board. Shingle the steak along the turnip purée. In the center, place a small mound of sautéed turnip greens and randomly toss the barbequed sweetbreads around the greens. Place 2 small micro radishes on the corner of the plate.

Author's Note: Wondra Flour (made by Gold Medal) is a quick-mixing version of all-purpose flour, ideal for extra-creamy, lump-free gravies, and ultra-flaky and crispy pie crusts. It is made by a process of agglomeration of small flour particles to make a more uniform product. Its lightness also makes it perfect as the dredging flour for fish and poultry.

**Hakurei turnips are a Japanese variety sometimes referred to as the salad turnip, due to their crisp, delicious, raw flavor. They are as delicious raw as cooked.*

***Fleur de sel (literally "flower of salt") is the top layer of hand-harvested sea salt traditionally gathered in Brittany, on the west coast of France. For salt that is mined closer to home, see J.Q. Dickinson Salt-Works, page 211.*

"Making and enjoying good food is not a matter of class or wealth or education or race. It is a matter of heart."
—Liz Williams

Carolina Bison Sirloin
with Red Wine Butter & Stuffed Ulster Baked Potato

Paul Rankin & Nick Nairn

Another recipe from Ulster-Scots Chefs Rankin & Nairn, this recipe makes use of Carolina-raised bison steaks, as well as the staple ingredient of the Irish nation, the potato, known in Southern Appalachia as "tater," just as tomatoes are known as "maters" and tobacco as "baccer".

For the Steaks
1 bison rib loin
Olive oil for searing
Salt and pepper to taste

For the Red Wine Butter
300 grams (1¼ cup) unsalted
   butter, softened
1 clove garlic, crushed
2 shallots, finely chopped
200 milliliters (⅔ cup) red wine
2 tablespoons parsley, chopped
1 sprig thyme
Salt and pepper to taste

For the Stuffed Ulster Baked Potato
4 large baking potatoes
3 tablespoons heavy cream
2 egg yolks
2 tablespoons unsalted butter
3 spring onions, finely chopped
2 tablespoons olive oil
Salt and pepper to taste

For the Salad
Baby leaves of gem lettuce (a
   miniature variety of romaine)
Watercress
Rocket (arugula)
Mixed lettuce leaves
1 tablespoon olive oil
Salt and pepper to taste

For the Steaks

Portion the loin into even-sized steaks. Remove any excess fat and sinew from the steaks, and season well on both sides with salt and pepper. Heat a large frying pan and add olive oil, place the steaks in the pan, and cook for 2–3 minutes on each side to sear. Once seared, place the red wine butter on top and set in oven for 5–6 minutes until the butter has melted and the steak is tender.

For the Red Wine Butter

To make the butter, sweat the shallots, garlic, and thyme in a little butter. Add the red wine and reduce until sticky. Once sticky, remove from the heat, add the parsley, and allow to cool. Once cool, fold through the softened butter and set in the refrigerator.

For the Stuffed Ulster Baked Potato

Place the potatoes in a large oven tray, drizzle with olive oil, and season with salt and pepper. Place in the oven at 400°F for 30 minutes, until soft.

Remove potatoes from the oven and set aside until cool enough to handle. Halve, scoop out the insides, and put through a potato ricer.

In a small pan, add the cream, butter, and seasonings, and heat until the butter has melted. Pour the cream mixture over the potatoes, and stir until smooth.

Finish the potato mixture with the spring onions and whipped egg yolks. Place the potato mixture into a piping bag and pipe back into the skins ready for baking. Repeat this with all the skins and place in the oven at 180°C (350°F) for 15 minutes until golden on top.

For the Salad

Separate the baby gem leaves and mix together with the watercress, rocket (arugula), and other leaves. Drizzle with olive oil and season with salt and pepper, toss well together, and place in a bowl ready for serving.

To Serve

Place the bison-buttered steak off-center and place the baked potato to one side. Serve flanked by the mixed salad.

PotLikker Soup

Denny Trantham

A great soup for a winter's day, this recipe is sure to warm your heart and stick to your ribs!

2 (1-pound) smoked ham hocks
1 medium onion, chopped
1 medium carrot, diced
1 tablespoon bacon grease
1 garlic clove, chopped
½ cup dry white wine
½ teaspoon salt
¼ teaspoon dried crushed
   red pepper
1 (14½-ounce) can vegetable
   broth
½ (16-ounce) package fresh
   collard greens, washed,
   trimmed, and chopped

Bring ham hocks and 8 cups water to a boil in a Dutch oven over medium-high heat. Boil 5 minutes; drain. Reserve hocks; wipe Dutch oven clean.

Sauté onion and carrot in hot oil in Dutch oven over medium heat 4 to 5 minutes or until tender; add garlic, and cook 1 minute. Add wine; cook, stirring occasionally, 2 minutes or until wine is reduced by half.

Add hocks, 8 cups water, salt, and crushed red pepper to onion mixture, and bring to a boil. Cover, reduce heat to low, and simmer 3 hours or until ham hocks are tender.

Remove hocks, and let cool 30 minutes. Remove meat from bones; discard bones. Transfer meat to an airtight container; cover and chill. Cover remaining ingredients in Dutch oven with lid, and chill soup 8 hours.

Skim and discard fat from soup in Dutch oven. Stir in meat and vegetable broth. Bring mixture to a boil. Gradually stir in collards. Reduce heat, and simmer, stirring occasionally, 45 to 50 minutes or until collards are tender.

~

"The fountain of youth is in your kitchen."
—PARAPHRASED FROM DR. JOHN LaPUMA

Ample Sides

Accoutrements to enhance and dance alongside
the centerpiece

An American folksong which, according to Alan Lomax, musicologist and folklorist formerly of the Library of Congress, was originally associated with African slaves brought from Niger. "Bile" does not refer to that greenish matter found next to the liver; it simply means "boil." Hoecakes are cornmeal cakes baked originally on a hoe over an open fire, and these days in a skillet.

Bile 'Em Cabbage Down

(Traditional)

Went up on the mountain
Just to give my horn a blow
Thought I heard my true love say
Yonder comes my beau

Wisht I had a nickel
Wisht I had a dime
Wisht I had a pretty little girl
To love me all the time

Possum in a 'simmon tree
Raccoon on the ground
Raccoon says you son-of-a-gun
Shake some 'simmons down

Someone stole my old 'coon dog
Wish they'd bring him back
He chased the big hogs through the
    fence
And the little ones through the crack

Once I had an old gray mule
His name was Simon Slick
He'd roll his eyes and back his ears
And how that mule would kick

How that mule would kick
He kicked with his dying breath
He shoved his hind feet down his
    throat
And kicked himself to death

Took my gal to the blacksmith shop
To have her mouth made small
She turned around a time or two
And swallowed shop and all

Possum is a cunnin' thing
He travels in the dark
And never thinks to curl his tail
Till he hears old Rover bark

I bought my gal a bicycle
She learned to ride it well
She ran into a telephone pole
And busted it all to pieces

Bile 'em cabbage down, boys
Bake them hoecakes brown
The only song that I can sing
Is bile 'em cabbage down

Leather Britches

Bill Best

Leather Britches, also called shucky beans, shuck beans, and in some areas, fodder beans, are made from full green beans which have been strung, broken into pieces, and then dried. Traditionally they are dried by running a needle and thread through each piece and hanging them up in long strings behind a wood cook stove to dry out as quickly as possible. They can also be dried by spreading them out in a greenhouse on bed sheets, newspapers, or window screens. Still another way of drying them is putting them on window screens on a tin roof and bringing them in at night, or even putting them in a junk car with windows rolled up on sunny days. Once eaten almost every day during winter and spring, they are now served mostly on special days such as family reunions, weddings, anniversaries, Thanksgiving, Christmas, New Year, and other holidays. Drying beans is the oldest way of preserving them and still very effective. Properly dried and cooked, they are delicious.
—B. Best

Author's Note: My parents preserved beans this way when I was a child. My earliest memories revolve around planting and harvesting and preserving, with less emphasis put on eating, a detail which was destined to change as I grew older. My parents strung, but left the beans whole rather than breaking them into pieces as Bill advises. While the whole bean might be a little more challenging to eat with finesse, it looks mighty fine ornamenting whatever dish you might prepare, as an accent or as a full side course. "Leather Britches" is also the title of a rousing fiddle tune.

A mess of full, tender heirloom string beans (no stringless varieties; Little Greasies, Cornfield beans and Cut-Shorts are ideal; Shelly beans are problematic, as they tend to fall apart)*

1 ham hock
Salt and pepper to taste

Author's Note: A "mess of beans" means a quantity sufficient for one meal, or for a particular occasion. It is a vague amount that depends on the harvest of the moment, the number of guests, and the appetite of the particular guests, plus how much you might want to have left over. The term can be applied to greens as well.

Soak overnight (8 P.M. to 8 A.M.). Then pour water off and soak again from 8 A.M. until noon.

Pour water off a second time and soak through the noon hour.

Pour water off a third time and then cook the same way as you would cook green beans. (These three periods of soaking do not require a lot of monitoring that might interfere with regular work at home. Other people use different time frames, but this works for me.)

For cooking, my mother used chunks of salt-cured side meat. My wife uses several strips of uncooked bacon. Bob Perry, University of Kentucky chef, uses a ham hock.

Cook until tender and serve with butter, cornbread, and diced onions.

Grandma Cora's Sweet & Sour Pickles

Marty Lewis

This recipe can be made with just a few of the ingredients below or with a whole basketful. Dose the tomatoes and onions to taste according to how many cucumbers you have.

Pickling cucumbers, cut
   lengthways in spears
Equal thirds of sugar, water,
   and vinegar, to cover
   cucumbers
Green tomatoes, quartered
Onions, quartered
Whole cayenne peppers to taste
A couple tablespoons pickling
   spice (mustard seeds, pepper
   corns, dill seeds)

Bring water, vinegar, sugar, and pickling spices (enough to cover ingredients in jars) to boil. Arrange cucumbers, tomatoes, peppers, and onions in clean mason jars. Fill jars to bottom of neck with pickling liquid. Attach lids. When cool, check to be sure lids have sealed.

Chow Chow

Joe Scully

1 medium head Napa cabbage,
  chopped
1 cup onions, chopped
1 cup green tomatoes, chopped
  (about 4)
1 stalk celery
1 cup green bell pepper
  (about 4)
½ cup red bell pepper (about 2)
1½ tablespoons salt
1¼ cups vinegar
¾ cup sugar
1 teaspoon dry mustard
½ teaspoon turmeric
¼ teaspoon ground ginger
¼ teaspoon crushed red pepper

Combine chopped vegetables and sprinkle with salt. Let stand 4 to 6 hours in a cool place. Drain well. Combine vinegar, sugar, and spices in a pot, and simmer 10 minutes. Add macerated vegetables and simmer 10 minutes.

Cool and store for up to three weeks in the refrigerator.

"The fabric of our lives is bound in the food that we eat and the way we sit down to eat."
—Maira Kalman

Hoppin' John

Denny Trantham

1 diced onion
2 tablespoons bacon drippings
1 (8½-ounce) package ready-to-
   serve jasmine rice
2 cups cooked and drained
   black-eyed peas
Salt and pepper to taste

Sauté diced onion in bacon drippings in a large skillet over medium-high heat, 5 minutes or until golden. Stir in rice and black-eyed peas; cook, stirring gently, 5 minutes or until thoroughly heated. Add salt and pepper to taste.

"One of the very nicest things about life is the way we must regularly stop whatever it is we are doing and devote our attention to eating."
—LUCIANO PAVAROTTI AND WILLIAM WRIGHT

Moonshine-Preserved Meyer Lemons Makes about 2 quarts

Denny Trantham

This is a fantastic use for any of those dubious jars of spirits you may have at the back of your cupboard!

10–12 Meyer lemons
Coarse sea salt
Moonshine (legal, of course!)

Wash and dry the lemons thoroughly. Remove any green points attached to the ends of the lemons. Cut them in quarters lengthwise. Place 2–3 pieces in a clean, wide-mouth quart-sized glass jar. Top with a thick layer of salt. Repeat: lemon, salt, lemon, salt, and so on, all the way to the top, pressing down hard as you go to draw out the juice. Don't worry if the juices don't appear immediately; they soon will, with all that salt. The lemons should be totally submerged by their own juice, and reach all the way to the top of the jar. Top with an extra layer of salt to ensure that no lemon skin is exposed (or it may mold). Put the lids on the jars and close tightly.

Place the jars in a dark, cool place. They will be ready in two weeks, at which point they should be refrigerated. At this point, gently rinse the lemons and replace liquid with moonshine (or whatever favorite spirit you may desire). Store the jar of lemons in the refrigerator.

To use, take out a quarter of a lemon at a time. Discard the pulp (or put it back in the jar to use later), rinse the skin thoroughly, and mince the skin. Add to fish and chicken dishes, bean soups, salads and salsas.

Strawberry Jam

Denny Trantham

5 cups crushed strawberries
    (about 5 pounds)
¼ cup lemon juice
6 tablespoons pectin
7 cups granulated sugar
8 half-pint glass preserving jars
    with lids and bands

Prepare boiling water canner. Heat jars in simmering water until ready for use. Do not boil. Wash lids in warm soapy water and set bands aside.

Combine strawberries and lemon juice in a 6- or 8-quart saucepan. Gradually stir in pectin. Bring mixture to a full rolling boil that cannot be stirred down, over high heat, stirring constantly.

Add entire measure of sugar, stirring to dissolve. Return mixture to a full rolling boil. Boil hard for 1 minute, stirring constantly. Remove from heat. Skim foam if necessary.

Ladle hot jam into hot jars, leaving ¼ inch headspace. Wipe rim. Center lid on jar. Apply band until fit is fingertip tight.

Process in a boiling water canner for 10 minutes, adjusting for altitude. Remove jars and cool. Check lids for seal after 24 hours. Lid should not flex up and down when center is pressed.

Maple Apple Butter

Denny Trantham

4½ pounds apples
1 cup cider or apple juice
1 cup brown sugar
1 cinnamon stick
1 teaspoon allspice, ground
¼ cup maple syrup
7 half-pint glass preserving jars
   with lids and bands

Wash, quarter, and remove both stem and blossom ends from apples. Combine apples, apple cider, brown sugar, allspice and cinnamon sticks in large, deep, stainless steel sauce pan. Simmer, covered, until apples are soft, about 25 minutes.

Remove cinnamon sticks and reserve. Crush apples with potato masher. Put mixture through sieve or strainer to remove peels and seeds. Measure out 6 cups of apple-sauce, set aside.

Measure maple syrup; set aside.

Return apple purée (and, if you want, cinnamon stick for a more potent cinnamon flavor) to a clean, large, stainless steel saucepan and, stirring occasionally, bring to a boil. Reduce heat and boil gently for 1 hour or until apple spread mounds on a spoon or desired thickness is reached.

Add maple syrup and cook gently another 30 minutes, stirring often. When apple mixture has reached desired consistency, remove from heat.

Working with one jar at a time, remove hot jar from freshly run dishwasher and, using a funnel and a ladle, fill jars with apple butter. Remove a hot lid from water (set to soak before bringing jam to boil), using tongs, place on the jar, and screw on the screw band, finger tight.

Place on a clean towel on your counter and do not touch for 24 hours. Repeat with remaining jars until apple butter is finished. Jars will seal on their own. After 24 hours, test for seal. Sealed lids curve downward and do not move when pressed. If any have not sealed, place in refrigerator for immediate use.

Ramp Compound Butter

Mark Rosenstein

1½ pounds ramps, trimmed and
   cleaned
4 pounds unsalted butter, cut
   up and at room temperature
2 lemons, zested and juiced
Salt and pepper to taste
Thyme (optional)

Materials:
Parchment or waxed paper*
Freezer bags

As an alternative to using parchment, you can use all the leftover butter wrappers to make small logs. Plastic wrap can be used as well.

Author's Note: A sliver of ramp butter atop a freshly grilled steak would add extra life and zest!

Trim the ends off the ramps and clean them well under cold, running water. Blanch them quickly (30 seconds) by dropping the ramps in a large pot of salted, boiling water, and then shock them in ice water. Drain the ramps, squeezing as much liquid out as you can. With a sharp knife, thinly slice the ramps. In a large bowl (or KitchenAid with a paddle), mix well the butter, lemon juice, lemon zest, ramps, salt, and pepper. On sheets of parchment, form logs of butter of approximately ½ pound each, and roll the parchment tightly around the butter. Put the butter logs in two sets of freezer bags and seal tightly, removing all the air, and store in the freezer.

Pickled Chard Stems

Nate Allen

These work well as a garnish on any salad, entrée, or savory dessert because they add a unique flavor and a beautiful color. This is also a wonderful use for the often-discarded stem of the Swiss chard leaf.

Stems of Bright Lights Swiss chard, or Rainbow chard (the leaves are entirely edible as well and have a huge range of possible uses)

Equal parts sugar and salt to taste

Finely chop the chard stems to about ⅛–¼ inches in length. Blend with sugar and salt, and allow to rest for 15–20 minutes (dry pickling). Use immediately or store in refrigerator for 24 hours before serving.

"When you grow a vegetable yourself, you're less likely to boil it to death."

—Darina Allen, Ballymaloe Cookery School, Ireland

Basic Grits

Serves 4

Denny Trantham

2 cups water, 2 cups heavy cream
  or half & half
2 tablespoons butter
1 cup stone ground grits
Salt to taste

Combine water, salt, and butter and bring to a boil. Slowly add in the stone ground grits, return to a boil, then reduce to a simmer. Cook the grits, stirring occasionally so that that they do not stick, until they are creamy. This takes about 25 minutes, but you can cook them longer if you add more water.

Stone-Ground Cheese Grits

Serves 4

Denny Trantham

4 cups milk
¼ cup butter (½ stick)
1 cup stone ground grits
1 cup grated mild cheddar
  cheese
Salt and pepper to taste

Bring milk, butter, salt, and pepper to a boil. Add in the stone ground grits and reduce heat to a simmer. Stir often and until grits are thick and creamy. Stir in cheese and enjoy.

Grits, Basic and Beyond

Joe Scully

1 part stone ground grits
3 parts water
Heavy cream to taste
Salt and pepper to taste
Cheddar cheese to taste
   (optional)
Jalapeños, chopped, to taste
   (optional)

Bring the water to a boil. While boiling, sprinkle in the grits. Keep stirring until thoroughly combined. Simmer for around 25 minutes. Season and add cream. Add the cheddar and/or jalapeños if desired.

"Every chef should have to work on a farm for a year before setting foot in the kitchen."
—Darina Allen, Ballymaloe Cookery School, Ireland

Cracklin's & Grits

SG Séguret

If you've ever taken part in a hog killin', you know that cracklin's (cracklings) are what rises to the top of a kettle of lard that is being rendered down. Imbued with good hog fat, they melt on your tongue and make you almost scream for more. Atop creamy grits, there is nothing better in this world except a good cup of coffee to go along with them, and the love of a good man across the table.

Grits (dose according to hunger
    and number of people present)
Cracklin's, about a tablespoon
    per person
Knob of butter per person
Large grain salt and fresh
    ground pepper to taste
Sprinkling of fresh thyme or
    oregano (optional)
Nasturtium flowers (1 per
    person, optional)

Cook grits as directed (you can use either instant or slow-cook grits), while lightly sautéing cracklings until just crisp but not burnt (they tend to burn very quickly). Stir in a knob of butter and add a sprinkling of large-grain sea salt and a grinding of pepper to taste. Top with cracklin's, still hot from the pan, and with chopped herbs or nasturtium flowers if desired. Nasturtiums go particularly well with grits, and are splendidly colorful as well, but just plain butter and cracklin's are really all you need.

Poke Sallet

SG Séguret

Poke sallet has long been a staple in the Appalachian South. As Southern Food-ways Alliance member Joe York says, "It's free and you don't even have to plant it or weed it," adding, "Some people can't live without it once they've tasted it."

In 1968 Tony Joe White wrote and recorded "Poke Salad Annie," which was later covered by Elvis, and featured some spectacular moves and classic Elvis expressions that make you want to go out and gather a mess this instant:

Every day for supper time, she'd
    go down by the truck patch
And pick her a mess of poke salad,
    and carry it home in a tow
    sack

Polk salad Annie, the 'gators got
    your granny
Everybody says it was a shame
'Cause her momma was a-workin'
    on the chain gang

—Tony Joe White

Pailful young poke leaves
Lots of salted water
A couple tablespoons bacon fat

Wash and parboil the poke leaves (*Phytolacca americana*), removing any stems and berries that may have fallen into the bucket. Pour off the water, and parboil a second and (optionally) third time to be certain that any toxins have been removed. (If you have gathered young leaves without a trace of purple, you are probably safe from any serious toxicity.)

Strain and sauté in bacon fat, and serve alongside chicken or pork, and mashed potatoes. Top, if you are lucky enough to have them, with sautéed ramps.

Gravies & Sauces

That little bit of extra zest

This popular ballad was written by Madison County, North Carolina's Bascom Lamar Lunsford, known as the "Minstrel of the Appalachians." Over the years, he recorded more than 3,000 songs for the Library of Congress and the Columbia University Library. He also performed at the White House for the King and Queen of Great Britain. In 1928, he started the Mountain Dance and Folk Festival in Asheville, North Carolina. Still held annually, it is recognized as the first event in the country to be labeled "Folk Festival." His original recording of "Good Old Mountain Dew," which he sold for the money for a bus ticket, was used as the first advertising theme for the then newly created Mountain Dew soda.

Mountain Dew

Bascom Lamar Lunsford

Down the road here from me there's
    an old holler tree
Where you lay down a dollar or two
If you hush up your mug, then they'll
    give you a jug
Of that good old mountain dew

Well, they call it that good old
    mountain dew,
And them that refuse it are few.
I'll hush up my mug if you'll fill up
    my jug
With that good old mountain dew

My brother Bill runs a still on the
    hill
Where he turns out a gallon or two
And the buzzards in the sky get so
    drunk they can't fly

Just from smellin' that good old
    mountain dew

My Uncle Mort, he is sawed off and
    short,
He measures 'bout four foot two,
But he thinks he's a giant when you
    give him a pint
Of that good old mountain dew

Old Auntie June had a brand new
    perfume,
It had such a sweet smellin' "pew"
But imagine her surprise, when she
    had it analyzed,
It was nothin' but that good old
    mountain dew

I know a guy named Pete, his hair is
    never neat
Though he dips it in syrup and glue,
But it always stays in place with just
    a little trace
Of that good old mountain dew

The preacher walked by, with his
    head heisted high
Said his wife had been down with
    the flu

And he said that I ort just to give
    him a quart
Of that good old mountain dew

Well, you take a little trash and you
    mix it up with ash,
And the sole of an old worn out shoe
Then you stir it awhile with an old
    rusty file,
And you call it that good old
    mountain dew.

*"You can tell a lot about a culture from its cuisine: what it values,
what challenges it faces. In Appalachia, where people have lived off
the land for centuries, it was common practice to 'eat local' way before
that was cool. Now that the rest of the world is trying to do the same,
people are looking anew at this region's cooking. Instead of seeing it
as a food of poverty, some are suggesting it's an undiscovered gem in
American regional cooking."*
—Robbie Harris

Apple Cider Walnut Vinaigrette

Mark Rosenstein

¼ cup coarsely chopped walnuts

1 teaspoon butter

1½ teaspoons salt

2 large shallots, peeled and
 halved

2 tablespoons apple cider
 vinegar

2 teaspoons sugar

½ teaspoon white pepper

1 teaspoon Dijon mustard

1 cup olive oil

Roast walnuts until lightly brown. Remove from oven, and stir in butter and salt. In food processor, grind shallots one at a time. Add vinegar, sugar, pepper, and mustard. Drizzle oil in very slowly. Add the walnuts, and process for a few seconds.

"Life is so brief that we should not glance either too far backwards or forwards...therefore study how to fix our happiness in our glass and in our plate."
—Grimod de la Reynière

Cider Almond Dressing

Makes 3 cups

Mark Rosenstein

1¼ cups blanched almonds
10 tablespoons light salad oil
10 tablespoons fresh apple cider
½ cup cider vinegar
6 tablespoons honey
½ teaspoon salt

Combine all ingredients in a blender, and purée until smooth.

"Food to the cook is just like marble to Michelangelo: it is up to the artist to bring out what is already there."
—Unknown

Imogene's Chocolate Gravy

Sherry Lewis

This recipe is delicious and our family has enjoyed it for generations. It's very simple; just sugar, cocoa, and milk. We don't even use measurements; just more sugar and cocoa than milk. You could use the recipe for making the old fashioned fudge and boil it until it makes a thickened syrup (no flour, butter, or vanilla). It's great on biscuits and pancakes.
—*S. Lewis*

Sugar

Cocoa

Milk

Author's Note: If you wish to turn this into hot chocolate, just add more milk. You can always throw in a little vanilla too, and even a touch of cinnamon if you like that extra note.

Combine ingredients in a saucepan (more sugar and cocoa, in ratio to taste, than milk). Boil until it reaches the consistency desired and pour over freshly baked biscuits or pancakes.

"Magical dishes, magical words: A great cook is, when all is said and done, a great poet."
—Marcel Grancher

Pan Gravy

SG Séguret

This is the simplest gravy in the world, and can be made in a few moments, enhancing any meat dish which might otherwise come across too dry. If your meat has been properly seasoned, there will be no need of additional seasoning. If, however, you feel it is needed, you can throw in a smidgen of pepper and salt, being careful not to salt too much.

Pan drippings from meat source
Liquid (broth, beer, water, or
    wine)

Remove meat, when ready, to the plate or platter on which it will be served, add your liquid to the hot pan and stir with a wooden spoon until all the goodness of the meat has been incorporated in the liquid. Pour bubbling hot onto the meat to be served. If you're looking for more refinement, you can pour the sauce through a sieve, and can even serve it in a sauceboat, but sometimes the little bits that remain behind add to the character of the dish, particularly if you're wishing to stay true to the honored rugged Appalachian spirit.

Biscuit Gravy

SG Séguret

No self-respecting Southerner would ever turn up his nose at a biscuit smothered in gravy, hot and steaming and redolent of whatever meat is to be served alongside, be it bacon, sausage, or country-style ham. The process begins like making a roux (flour stirred into fat, with a liquid added). Here, milk is the liquid of choice, and you must be standing by, spoon or whisk in hand, ready to stir vigorously as soon as you pour it in.

Pan drippings from bacon or
   sausage or country-style ham
Extra oil if needed

1 tablespoon flour
Salt and pepper to taste

Make certain you have sufficient fat in your pan so that your gravy won't immediately be too dry. A couple of tablespoons, depending on how many you are serving, is usually sufficient. Add flour and stir or whisk around immediately until flour and fat form a smooth paste. Continue cooking for a few moments until the flour flavor cooks away. I like to add my seasoning (salt, pepper, a few red pepper flakes, possibly some chopped sage or fresh thyme leaves) at this point. Add milk gradually and stir away lumps that may form. Keep adding milk until desired consistency is reached, remembering that the gravy will continue to thicken slightly when removed from the pan. Check for seasoning and serve hot on a freshly split biscuit.

If you wish a more rustic consistency, you can stir a little cornmeal in with the flour or incorporate some crumbled sausage or bacon. This is known as "sawmill gravy," as its heartiness kept the ravenous sawmill workers going at the logging camps at the turn of the 20th century. In Kentucky, it was known as "poor-do," as it was a main staple with which the poor made do.

The same gravy can be made with chicken drippings and served with Sunday fried chicken, or on top of biscuits to accompany a chicken dish.

Daily Bread

The staff of life

Composition of "Walking in My Sleep" has been credited to Tennessee's Fiddlin' Arthur Smith, who recorded it in 1930, but the song was also recorded by several other performers in the 78 RPM era. Herman Johnson titled it "Just an Old Rag in G."

Walkin' in My Sleep

(Traditional)

Walkin' in my sleep, babe.
Walkin' in my sleep.
Up and down that Dixie line,
Walkin' in my sleep.

If you see that gal of mine tell her
   if you please
When she goes to bake her bread,
   roll up her dirty sleeves

Bake them biscuits baby, bake
   'em good and brown
When I eat my breakfast I'm
   Alabama bound

Pain in my finger, pain in my toe
Pain in my ankle bone, ain't
   gonna work no more

Susi's Super-Simple Biscuits

SG Séguret

When I was growing up, the nearest neighbor girl was slim and wiry. She was two years younger than I but she could run faster. She flew. I'm not sure exactly how she did it, because I, too, was a good runner. But no matter how well I started out in a race, leaning forward and going with all the speed of my young sinew, she always managed to slip ahead. Her feet knew no limit.

She was suntanned—a farmer's tan, people called it—with the mark of her shirt sleeves visible half-way up her arm. We saw each other only on Sundays because every other day of the week she had to help in the fields. Sometimes I would come over the narrow trail that ran through the woods between our two farms, and help her tie tomatoes or pick beans or strip tobacco plants.

It was hard work for a child of less than five years, but she knew nothing else. Her older sisters set out the young tobacco plants and walked along the tomato rows with a sprayer that carried deadly poison. They too knew nothing else.

When at last we were allowed to play, we climbed to the hayloft where we might see a blacksnake wriggle through a knothole, leaving his skin behind him. Sometimes we picked up old things we found lying around the barn's dusty floor, such as an empty medicine bottle which we would stuff with boxwood leaves.

We would also roll down the hill above her house, over and over, until we were so dizzy we couldn't stand, and our heads seemed to be our feet and our stomachs seemed to be our heads. The chickens had been scratching there, and we often came out of our rolling sessions with polka-dotted blouses, which didn't help our stomachs any.

What did help was to go down to the grape arbor and crawl underneath where the grapes hung covered with morning dew. We could eat until we were sick, and nobody would miss anything, there were so many of them. When we'd had our fill we'd run into the kitchen and pull open the drawer where we knew biscuits were kept. They were even better when they were a day old and just a little bit hard, smelling of self-rising flour.

Like my favorite chocolate cake recipe, I searched for years before I stumbled across one so simple and delicious that there has never been a contest since. (Thank you, Nathalie Dupree!) You can add all kinds of ingredients if you wish, but none here can be taken away. It's like jazz. When you strip out all the unnecessary notes, that's when you get to the bare bones of your melody. When you understand the backbone, then and only then will your embellishing make sense.

2 cups self-rising flour
(or 2 cups all-purpose flour and
   1 tablespoon baking powder)
1 teaspoon large grain salt (a bit
   less if using self-rising flour)
1 cup heavy cream

Preheat your oven to 425°F. Sift flour and leavening, if not using self-rising flour, into a bowl, or simply pour in and whisk around a time or two to fluff up. Add salt, pour in cream, and stir around rapidly with a fork until the mass clumps together into a ball. If it is too flaky, add a touch more cream. It should adhere without being soggy.

Flour hands, and pat out on a floured surface to a thickness of between ½ inch and ¾ inch. Fold dough over on itself and pat out again. Fold over one more time, pat out to preferred thickness, and cut into rounds with a biscuit cutter or an upside-down glass, dipped in flour.

Place biscuits side by side (touching) in a glass pie dish or in a cast iron skillet, and bake for 10–12 minutes until just browning on top.

Serve immediately with butter and fresh jam, molasses, or sausage and gravy.

Southern Cathead Biscuits

Denny Trantham

Here's another biscuit recipe, of which there are as many as there are cooks in the South. Anything with Denny's name to it, of course, has got to be good!

2 cups White Lily Enriched
    Unbleached Self-Rising Flour
4 ounces Crisco Baking Sticks
    All-Vegetable Shortening,
    chilled
4 ounces (1 stick) salted butter,
    chilled
¾ cups whole buttermilk
2 ounces butter, melted

Heat oven to 500°F. Coat baking sheet with nonstick cooking spray. Measure flour into large bowl. Cut in shortening and butter with pastry blender or 2 knives until crumbs are the size of peas. Blend in just enough milk with fork until dough leaves sides of bowl.

Turn dough onto lightly floured surface. Knead gently 2 to 3 times. Roll dough to ¾-inch thickness. Cut using floured 2-inch biscuit cutter. Place on prepared baking sheet 1 inch apart for crisp sides or almost touching for soft sides. Bake 10 minutes or until golden brown.

Brush melted butter onto tops of biscuits as they come out of the oven.

Susi's Southern Cornbread

SG Séguret

2 cups self-rising cornmeal (or
1 cup fresh-ground cornmeal,
1 cup all-purpose flour, and
1 tablespoon baking powder;
you can experiment with more
cornmeal and less flour, to
your liking)
1¼ cup milk or buttermilk, or
yogurt or sour cream mixed
with milk
¼ cup oil or melted butter or
bacon drippings
1 teaspoon large grain salt
(a bit less if using self-rising
cornmeal)
1 large fresh egg

Preheat your oven to 425°F. Heat a cast iron skillet and pour in enough oil to coat bottom and sides well. Mix up your batter with rapid strokes, and pour in hot skillet. Bake for a scant 20 minutes, and eat hot out of the oven with plenty of fresh butter.

Basic Quick Beer Bread

SG Séguret

When you find yourself without bread, here is a quick remedy for any meal. Experiment with using different beers and throwing in a few sunflower or other seeds. Or try brushing the top with a mixture of beer and flour or cornmeal for a crispier crust.

3 cups flour
3¾ teaspoons baking powder
1 bottle beer
1 tablespoon honey
2¼ teaspoons salt

Grease loaf pan. Combine flour, baking powder, salt, beer, and honey in large bowl, and stir together until well-mixed. Bake in preheated 350°F oven for 45 minutes. Turn on rack and cool.

"We lived very simply, but with all the essentials of life well understood and provided for — hot baths, cold champagne, new peas and old brandy."
—Winston Churchill

Tomato, Ramp, & Bacon Quick Bread

SG Séguret

1¼ cup flour

1 tablespoon baking powder

3 eggs

⅓ cup olive oil

⅓ cup milk

½ cup grated gruyère cheese

½ cup sun-dried tomatoes

2–4 ramps, lightly sautéed

½ pound bacon, crisped and crumbled

Salt and pepper to taste

Crisp bacon and set aside to drain. Chop and sauté ramps in bacon fat. Mix together wet ingredients, beginning with the eggs. Add the dry ingredients, chopped dried tomatoes, crumbled bacon, and sautéed ramps. Pour in greased baking dish, and bake in the oven at 350°F for 40 minutes, or until done.

"A work of art, particularly a culinary work of art, is also a simplification. The cook makes a choice, and retains those things that best express his idea."

—Hervé This

Sweet Tea & Sassafras

Appalachian beverages to savor and sip

This is one of the many songs I grew up with, while eating cornbread or drinking sassafras tea by the fire. It still evokes taste memories for me, as it does the living room of the log cabin my father and mother built in the early '60s, and the lingering scent of woodsmoke.

Cornbread and 'Lasses and Sassafras Tea

(Traditional)

Come along girls and listen to my
    noise
Don't you marry no Arkansas boys
Marry you a guy from Tennessee
And eat cornbread, and 'lasses and
    sassafras tea
Cornbread, molasses and sassafras
    tea

Well I've been all around this whole
    wide world
Eat a lotta cooking from a lotta
    pretty girls
But none so good as Tennessee
With its cornbread, and 'lasses and
    sassafras tea
Cornbread, molasses and sassafras
    tea

Well old Uncle Sam, he lived on
    a hill
He never did die and I guess he
    never will
Folks all think he's past 93
But the old man's happy as he can be
Eatin' cornbread, molasses and
    sassafras tea

Old Uncle Bill on his dying bed
Neighbors crowded 'round and then
    he said
My last request, just let be
Cornbread, and 'lasses and sassafras
    tea
Cornbread, molasses and sassafras
    tea

Strawberry-Basil Lemonade

Makes about 12 cups

Mary Collins-Shepard

For the Strawberry-Basil Syrup

1½ cups granulated sugar

1 cup water

1 pound strawberries, washed, hulled, and sliced ½-inch thick

¾ cup tightly packed basil leaves

For the Lemonade

8 cups cold water

2 cups lemon juice, chilled

½ pound strawberries, washed, hulled, and sliced ½-inch thick, for garnish

¼ cup tightly packed, blemish-free basil leaves, for garnish

Ice, several cubes per serving

Prepare the strawberry-basil syrup by placing the sugar and water in a medium saucepan over high heat and stirring until the sugar dissolves and the mixture comes to a boil. Add the strawberries, reduce the heat to medium low, and simmer until the strawberries have softened, about 10 minutes.

Remove from the heat, add the basil leaves, and stir to incorporate. Cool to room temperature, about 45 minutes. Strain through a fine-mesh strainer set over a medium bowl; discard the solids. Cover the syrup and refrigerate until ready to use.

Prepare the lemonade by pouring the water, lemon juice, and ½ cup of the strawberry-basil syrup into a 3-quart pitcher or punch bowl, and stir to combine. Taste and add additional strawberry-basil syrup as needed. Add ice, and garnish with the sliced strawberries and basil leaves.

Sparkling Rosemary Honey Lemonade

Mary Collins-Shepard

8 cups water (sparkling)
6 lemons, juiced
½ cup honey
2 four-inch sprigs rosemary
Ice (optional)

Warm honey on stovetop, add rosemary, cover, set aside until cool. Remove herb sprigs, add honey to water and lemon juice in pitcher. Chill. Enjoy.

Lavender Blueberry Lemonade

Serves 2–3

Debby Maugans

1 pint fresh blueberries
½ cup water
½ cup sugar
2 tablespoons fresh lavender
  flowers
Soda water or plain water, to
  taste

Place all ingredients in a medium saucepan. Bring to a boil, stirring until sugar melts. Reduce heat and simmer 3 minutes. Remove from heat; let cool to room temperature.

Press through a fine wire-mesh sieve into a small pitcher. Add juice of 2 fresh lemons; stir well and chill thoroughly.

To serve, pour 3 tablespoons syrup mixture over ice; add chilled club soda or cold water to taste.

Sweet Tea

SG Séguret

In the early 1900s, sweet tea was an item of luxury used as an exhibition of wealth due to the expensive nature of tea, ice, and sugar. In fact, the first sweet tea recipe has been traced back to the cookbook Housekeeping in Old Virginia, by Marion Cabell Tyree, published in 1879. Now the elixir is found in any self-respecting Southern restaurant or home, and is the liquid comfort food of many a soul.

South Carolina is the first place in the United States where tea was grown and is the only state to ever have produced tea commercially. Iced tea's popularity parallels the development of refrigeration and the commercial manufacture of pure ice, which were in place as early as the middle of the nineteenth century.

A Note about Southern Appalachian Tastebuds

Traditionally, the Appalachian people were hard-working and thrifty. The extra boost of sugar in sweet tea helped them get through a day in the fields, if sipped at lunch, and gave them a bit of extra pep to get the evening chores done or to shine at a frolic (traditional music or dance event).

Scott Jones, executive food editor at Southern Living magazine says, "Sweet tea has always been a substitute beverage for what wine was doing in other regions. The tannins from the tea cleanse your palate, there's sweetness from the sugar and then the acidity from the lemon. It goes well with a lot of food." Country music icon Dolly Parton proclaims that sweet tea is "the house wine of the South."

12 regular-sized tea bags (Lipton is fine; loose-leaf tea is fine too)

⅛ teaspoon baking soda

1 quart water

Sugar (¼ cup per quart, to taste, added before cooling)

1 quart ice cubes

Additional water to top off pitcher

Optional mint sprigs and/or lemon slices for garnish

There are several ways of preparing sweet tea. One is to steep, as indicated above, using lots of tea bags for a concentrated base. Another is to use fewer tea bags and steep them longer than the standard 5 minutes, or dilute the infusion with less water or ice, or not at all.

Any kind of tea will work (make it to suit your tastes), from the cheapest supermarket variety to the specialty shop's best loose leaf. You can throw in mint sprigs (or mint tea bags) when steeping to give it a fresher feel.

If you forget to sweeten the tea while hot, you can always make a simple syrup by dissolving sugar in hot water, and mix it with the unsweetened tea.

A pinch of baking soda neutralizes the tannins in black tea, giving it a smoother taste. It also helps counter potential cloudiness.

No matter whether you prefer very sweet, medium sweet, or just a little sweet, the sight of a tall pitcher, dripping coolness, clinking with ice cubes, and swimming with mint is enough to make an Appalachian heart sing.

"Appalachian food has been sustainable and organic for generations. We've been offering "farm to table" fare forever, without ever having to say so."

—FRED SAUCEMAN

Spicebush Tea

Serves 1 (increase ingredients for multiple servings)

SG Séguret

Spicebush (Lindera benzoin) is a member of the laurel family (Laurelaceae), along with cinnamon, sassafras, and bay laurel. Dried, powdered spicebush berries can be substituted for allspice. Spicebush bark can be used as a substitute for cinnamon. Revolutionary and Civil War soldiers substituted spicebush tea (made from the twigs) for coffee. Spicebush twigs can also be thrown in a stew to liven up the sauce. The young green leaves can be sautéed in combination with other greens to lend a special zing to a meal.

Handful of spicebush twigs
Water to cover
Sugar or honey to taste

Break the twigs into 1-inch (more or less) sections, tearing strips of bark off the sides as you go so that as much of the interior is exposed as possible. Line the bottom of a saucepan with the twigs and bark, add cold water to cover, and bring slowly to a boil. Turn off heat, cover, and allow to steep for 5–20 minutes or more, tasting occasionally to see if sufficient strength is reached. Strength will be dependent on the time of year, the ratio of twigs to water, and the length of time infused.

Add sugar or honey to taste, while hot, and savor either hot or cold with ice.

Sassafras Tea

SG Séguret

As a child, I often sipped sassafras tea, steeped from the dried shavings of the outer bark of sassafras root, reddish in color, fragrant, and fortifying. We had a whole holler full of sassafras saplings, so it was no threat to the landscape to pull one up. I was always fascinated by the trilogy of leaf patterns: one standard tear-drop shape, one three-pronged, and the third shaped like a mitten. When my hands were small, I would take two mitten-shaped leaves and sew the delicate tissue together and try to slip my fingers in without breaking the treasure. Inevitably the leaf would tear, but that didn't stop me from trying again and again. If you dry the leaves and crumble them, they become filé powder, and are a thickening ingredient for gumbo.

Handful of sassafras twigs or
   (preferably) root shavings
Water, to cover
Sugar or honey to taste

Break the twigs into 1-inch (more or less) sections, tearing strips of bark off the sides as you go so that as much of the interior is exposed as possible. Line the bottom of a saucepan with the twigs and bark (or throw in fresh or dried root shavings for better flavor), add cold water to cover, and bring slowly to a boil. Turn off heat, cover, and allow to steep for 5–20 minutes or more, tasting occasionally to see if desired strength is reached. Strength will be dependent on the time of year, the ratio of twigs or root shavings to water, whether the root shavings are fresh or dried, and the length of time infused.

Add sugar or honey to taste, while hot, and savor either hot or cold with ice.

Sweet Birch Tea

Serves 1 (increase ingredients for multiple servings)

SG Séguret

Sweet Birch (Betula lenta), or Black Birch (also known as Cherry Birch), yields, from its inner bark, oil of wintergreen. The sap of the species can be fermented with corn to produce birch beer. When twigs are steeped, they produce a refreshing tea, perfect as a spring tonic.

Handful of birch twigs
Water to cover
Sugar or honey to taste

Break the twigs into 1-inch (more or less) sections, tearing strips of bark off the sides as you go so that as much of the interior is exposed as possible. Line the bottom of a saucepan with the twigs and bark, add cold water to cover, and bring slowly to a boil. Turn off heat, cover, and allow to steep for 5–20 minutes or more, tasting occasionally to see if desired strength is reached. Strength will be dependent on the time of year, the ratio of twigs to water, and the length of time infused.

Add sugar or honey to taste, while hot, and savor either hot or cold with ice.

Finishing Touches for the Sweet Tooth

That perfect final note of taste

The first known version of "Short'nin' Bread" was written by poet James Whitcomb Riley in 1900. E.C. Perrow published the first folk version of this song in 1915, collected in East Tennessee. The Beach Boys recorded it numerous times, notably on their 1979 album L.A. (Light Album).

Short'nin' Bread

(Traditional)

Three little children, layin' in bed
Two were sick and the other 'most
    dead
Called for the doctor and the doctor
    said,
Feed them children some short'nin'
    bread.

Mama's little baby loves short'nin',
    short'nin',
Mama's little baby loves short'nin'
    bread,
Mama's little baby loves short'nin',
    short'nin',
Mama's little baby loves short'nin'
    bread.

Put on the skillet, slip on the lid,
Mama's gonna make a little
    short'nin' bread,
That ain't all she's gonna do,
Mama's gonna make a little
    coffee, too.

When them children, sick in bed,
Heard that talk about short'nin'
    bread,
Popped up, well, to dance and sing,
Skipped around and cut the pigeon
    wing.

Aunt Jan's Prune Cake

Katie Hoffman and Maria Tiller

Prune Cake. It doesn't sound very elegant or interesting, does it? Don't be fooled! We made three different old-fashioned cakes one weekend in a frenzy of recipe-testing, and we took all three to Sunday dinner with the family. This particular recipe was given to Mamaw Tiller by her sister, Jan Kiser. It was the unanimous favorite in a household where there are very strong opinions about food. We tried another recipe for prune cake that was closely related to this one, but it had clearly been tinkered to make it more convenient. Instead of going to the trouble of chopping and cooking the prunes, as we did here, someone decided to use prune baby food as a substitute for the reconstituted dried prunes. Served side by side, there was no contest. The baby food cake was good, but this one blew it out of the water. This pan was empty when we left to head home from Sunday dinner, while the other still held half of a cake.
—*K. Hoffman*

2 cups pitted prunes, very finely
    chopped (about 14 ounces, or 2
    medium bags)
⅓ cup water (you may need
    to add more as the mixture
    cooks)
2 cups all-purpose flour
1 teaspoon soda
½ teaspoon salt
1 teaspoon cinnamon
1 teaspoon allspice
1 cup vegetable oil
3 eggs
1½ cups sugar
1–1½ teaspoons vanilla

For the Buttermilk Sauce
1 beaten egg
½ cup buttermilk
1 cup packed brown sugar
½ cup butter, either softened or
    melted and cooled a little
1 teaspoon vanilla
½ teaspoon soda
Remainder of the cooked prunes

Preheat oven to 350°F and grease and flour a 9x13-inch pan. There are cooked prunes in both the cake batter and the buttermilk sauce. It saves time if you cook them all together in a medium-sized saucepan before beginning the cake.

Begin by cooking the chopped prunes in the water over low or medium-low heat until they form a paste. It should still be easy to stir, but thick and fairly smooth. Set this aside to cool a bit as you make the cake batter. Whisk together the dry ingredients in a large bowl. In another large bowl (one that is big enough to eventually hold the finished batter), beat together the oil, sugar and eggs, adding the eggs one at a time, and beating well after adding each egg.

When the mixture is well-blended, measure out half of the cooked prune mixture and stir it into the wet ingredients. Beat this until it is fluffy. Add about a third of the dry ingredients to the wet, then alternate with buttermilk until done. Blend well after each addition, being careful to scrape the bottom of the bowl. Add the vanilla.

Pour the batter into the prepared pan and bake for 30–40 minutes. Test after 30 minutes. As the cake finishes baking, make the buttermilk sauce to go over it. We begin making the sauce about 10 or 15 minutes before the cake comes out of the oven.

For the Buttermilk Sauce
In a large saucepan, combine all the ingredients. Cook over low or medium-low heat until thickened, about 5–10 minutes. Pour the sauce over the warm cake and let sit until cool.

"Summer cooking implies a sense of immediacy, a capacity to capture the essence of the fleeting moment."
—Elizabeth David

Molassie Cake

Katie Hoffman

When I married into the Tiller family, I married into a treasure trove of old-fashioned recipes for cakes and desserts. My husband's grandfather, John Bernard Tiller of Lebanon, Virginia, made this homey cake from "molassies" (sweet sorghum syrup) that he "stirred off" with friends and family. Now, we depend on my father-in-law to seek out sorghum syrup from church fundraisers, where it's still made the old-fashioned way, with everyone taking a turn at the stir. This recipe came from my mother-in-law's handwritten stash of family favorites. In her notes, there's a recipe for butterscotch sauce. I've included the sauce recipe here, but we prefer this gingerbread-like cake unadorned or with a dollop of fresh whipped cream and a drizzle of sorghum for garnish. Without sauce, the cake ages well. In fact, it's even better the second or third day than the first.
—K. Hoffman

2½ cups all-purpose flour
1½ teaspoons baking soda
1 teaspoon salt
1 teaspoon cinnamon
1 teaspoon cloves
½ teaspoon powdered ginger

For the Sorghum Mixture
1 cup "molassies" (sweet sorghum syrup)
½ cup melted butter (the original recipe calls for Crisco)
½ cup sugar
2 eggs

For the Butterscotch Sauce
1½ cups brown sugar
⅔ cup corn syrup
4 tablespoons butter
¾ cup evaporated milk

Preheat oven to 375°F and grease and flour a 9x13-inch pan. In a large bowl, whisk together the dry ingredients. Add the sorghum mixture and stir. Then, at the last minute, stir in 1 cup boiling water. The batter will be very thin. Pour it into the greased and floured cake pan. Bake for about 30 minutes. Use a cake tester to determine doneness. Do not overbake. (Or if you do, make the butterscotch sauce and no one will ever know!)

For the Butterscotch Sauce
Bring sugar, syrup, and butter to a boil, then let cool. Add the milk slowly, stirring constantly. Pour evenly over the top of the warm cake. Much of the sauce will sink in, but you will get a beautiful shiny glaze over the top. Unlike the plain version, a glazed molassie cake doesn't keep more than two or three days.

Grilled Clanton Peach Cast Iron Cobbler

James Boyce

The town of Clanton, in Chilton County, is Alabama's "Peach Central," and even sports a giant water tank in the form of a peach, designed, bizarrely, by Chicago Bridge and Iron Company. Clanton is a town in central Alabama that celebrates it peaches as well as their season. They are usually the first of the season to arrive at market, and are therefore first on the menu. They are usually a bit smaller than regular peaches, with a beautiful taste and texture.

6 ripe Clanton (or other) peaches
1 tablespoon olive oil
2 sprigs fresh thyme, chopped
3 cups all-purpose flour
2 tablespoons sugar
1 tablespoon baking powder
½ teaspoon baking soda
1 teaspoon salt
1 stick butter
1 large egg
1¼ cups heavy cream

Pre-heat grill. Wash and cut peaches in half; remove pit. Place in bowl with oil and thyme, and toss. Place peaches on grill, cut side down, and grill for 3 minutes. Turn and cook for an additional 3 minutes. Remove, and keep at room temperature.

Assembly:
Heat oven to 375°F. Put the dry ingredients in a bowl. Combine, then cut in butter. In separate bowl, add egg to the cream and stir with a fork to combine. Make small well in dry mix of ingredients, and pour in cream mixture. Stir lightly until mixture is just combined. It should be loose. If necessary, add a small amount of cream.

Flour counter, and place dough on counter. With floured hands, form dough in a rectangle and fold in thirds (business letter style). Lay dough on top of fruit that's been placed in a 9x13-inch baking dish. Brush with cream and a sprinkling of sugar. Bake until golden brown, 20–25 minutes.

Rose Geranium Pound Cake with Blueberry Lavender Syrup

Mary Collins-Shepard

For the Cake

10–12 organic rose geranium leaves, stems removed

1½ cups unsalted butter, softened

2¼ cups sugar

1 teaspoon vanilla

5 eggs, left at room temperature for 30 minutes

3 cups sifted flour

¾ teaspoon baking powder

¼ teaspoon salt

¾ cup whole milk, at room temperature

Zest of 1 lemon

Additional rose geranium leaves for garnish

For the Blueberries in Syrup

¾ cup water

½ cup sugar

4 teaspoons dried edible lavender flowers or 2 tablespoons fresh edible lavender flowers

2 teaspoons fresh lemon juice

10 ounces blueberries (1 pint)

Grease and flour a 10-inch Bundt or tube cake pan. Place geranium leaves face down on bottom of pan, overlapping some, as needed, to fill in completely. Preheat oven to 325°F.

Cream butter and sugar with electric mixer until light and fluffy. Add vanilla, then eggs, one at a time, beating well between each addition. Add flour alternately with milk, beating well. Stir in lemon zest.

Pour batter into prepared cake pan, smoothing top. Bake 1–1¼ hours. If necessary to prevent over-browning (ovens vary), place a piece of aluminum foil lightly over the cake toward the end of baking. After cake is removed from oven, cool for 10 minutes and invert carefully on a plate. Peel away the leaves to reveal their imprints. Cool cake completely and dust lightly with confectioners' sugar.

For the blueberry syrup, bring water and sugar to a boil in a small saucepan, stirring until sugar is dissolved. Remove from heat and stir in lavender, then steep 30 minutes for dried lavender, or 40 minutes for fresh. Pour syrup through a fine-mesh sieve into a bowl, discarding lavender. Stir in lemon juice and blueberries.

Slice cake and serve with blueberry-lavender syrup. Garnish with fresh rose geranium leaf.

Aunt Cora's Pound Cake

Debby Maugans

My 102-year-old aunt Cora has called this cake her Christmas, birthday, wedding, and even funeral pound cake.

Her pound cake is a true old-fashioned version that calls for 1 pound of flour, 1 pound of butter, 1 pound of eggs, and not quite 1 pound of sugar. Its fragrance of nutmeg is soothing. The dense, buttery texture and sugary, crumbly top crust forms the standard by which I judge other pound cakes. But then, I may be biased by memories.

This is the recipe I found on a recent visit to my aunt. The family had been looking all over for her recipe, and I discovered it taped to the inside of a kitchen cabinet, located just above the decades-old mixer.
—D. Maugans

3¾ cups Old Mill unbleached
    plain flour
½ teaspoon freshly ground
    nutmeg
¾ teaspoon salt
4 sticks (1 pound) unsalted
    butter, softened
3 cups sugar
10 large eggs
2 teaspoons vanilla extract
Grated rind of 1 lemon

Preheat oven to 325°F. Grease and flour a 10-inch tube pan. Combine the cake flour, nutmeg, and salt, and sift into a medium bowl.

Cream butter and shortening in a large mixing bowl at highest speed of electric stand mixer until fluffy, scraping sides of bowl often, about 1 minute. Add sugar and beat until light and fluffy, scraping bowl as necessary, about 5 minutes. Add eggs, two at a time, beating at medium-low speed just until blended. Beat in extract.

Gradually add flour to creamed mixture, beating just until batter is well blended. Scrape into prepared tube pan and smooth top. Bake until a toothpick inserted in center comes out clean, about 1 hour 20 minutes to 1 hour 25 minutes.

Let cake cool in pan on wire rack until cool enough to handle. Loosen edges with thin sharp knife, remove pan, and turn out onto platter.

Southern Fried Pies

Denny Trantham

For the Fruit
¼ cup (half a stick) unsalted butter
¼ cup granulated sugar
2 Granny Smith apples, peeled, cored, and chopped (about 2 cups)
1 tablespoon brown sugar
¼ teaspoon ground nutmeg
½ teaspoon ground cinnamon

For the Homemade Dough
2½ cups self-rising flour, divided
½ cup vegetable shortening (Crisco)
2 tablespoons granulated sugar
1 egg yolk
½ cup ice water
1 cup vegetable oil, for the skillet
Powdered sugar or granulated sugar, for dusting (optional)

For the fruit, melt the butter and sugar together; add chopped apples and simmer, covered, over medium heat for about 15 to 20 minutes. Remove from heat, sprinkle brown sugar, nutmeg, and cinnamon over the apples, stir, taste, and adjust sweetness. Set aside to cool.

For the dough, cut the shortening into 2 cups of the flour. Stir in the sugar, egg yolk, and ice water until dough is sticky. Turn out onto a floured surface and sprinkle more flour on top, working it in until dough is smooth. Roll out to about ⅛- to ¼-inch-thick and cut into 4- to 6-inch circles. You may also pinch off golf ball-sized pieces and flatten individually by hand. Place about a half tablespoon of the cooled filling in the center of each round. Barely wet the edges of the round with water, fold over, lightly press down on the edges and the filling; seal the edges with the tines of a fork. Place all of the pies in a single layer onto a plate that has been lightly sprinkled with flour and refrigerate about 10 minutes.

Fry in a skillet, with about a ½ inch of hot oil, until browned on both sides. Remove from the skillet, drain on paper towels, and sprinkle with granulated sugar or dust with powdered sugar while still warm, if desired. Best served warm, but delicious cold too!

Cook's Notes
Oil must be hot (at least 350°F) or dough will absorb too much grease and will disintegrate.

If you use dried fruit

Combine 2 small packages (about 7 ounces each) of dried fruit in 2 cups of water and 1 cup of sugar in a heavy saucepan. Bring to a boil, reduce heat, and simmer about 20 minutes. Add seasonings and proceed. Can also use peaches, apricots, mixed or other dried or fresh fruits.

If you deep fry

Preheat deep fryer to 375°F and fry, in batches to avoid chilling the oil, for about 3½ minutes, or until golden brown. Shake basket gently after about 30 seconds to keep the pastry from sticking.

If you bake them

Preheat oven to 400°F. Place the mini pies on a greased cookie sheet or pan. Make a couple of small slits in the dough so the steam will vent out, brush the tops with the juice from the pan or with an egg wash over each pie if desired, and sprinkle tops with a bit of granulated sugar. Bake in a 400°F oven for about 20 minutes, or until golden brown.

For Peach Filling: For peach pies, or other juicy fruit such as pears, peel, and chop ripe peaches. (You'll want about 2 pounds.) Set aside in a colander and let them drain for at least 30 minutes, then sprinkle with ¼ cup of sugar before filling dough. It is not necessary to stew these softer fruits, so long as they are ripe, although you may if you prefer. You can also substitute any other stewed fruit for pie recipe.

For Strawberry Filling: Add 2 cups of hulled and mashed strawberries to a saucepan, add ¼ cup granulated sugar. Taste and increase sugar as needed, as strawberries will vary in sweetness. Mix 2 tablespoons of cornstarch with 1 tablespoon of water and add to the mixture. Bring to a boil and cook until mixture thickens. Set aside to cool completely.

For Blackberry Filling: Add ½ pint of fresh blackberries or 1 (21-ounce) can, drained, to a saucepan, along with ¼ cup of granulated sugar. Taste and increase sugar as needed, as berries will vary in sweetness. Add 2 teaspoons of fresh lemon juice and a pinch of the zest. Mix 2 tablespoons of cornstarch with 1 tablespoon of water and add to the mixture. Bring to a boil and cook until mixture thickens. Remove and mash the berries to desired consistency.

For Sweet Potato Filling: Combine 2 cups of mashed, cooked sweet potatoes, with ½ cup (1 stick) of softened butter, a cup of light brown sugar, packed, a pinch of salt, and ½ teaspoon each of cinnamon and nutmeg, and enough milk to moisten. Can also be made with leftover candied yams and sweet potato casserole.

For Chocolate Filling: Combine 2 cups of granulated sugar with 6 tablespoons of cocoa powder (like Hershey's). Add in ½ cup (1 stick) of melted butter.

Southern Sweet Potato Praline Spoonbread

Denny Trantham

2½ cups heavy cream
1 teaspoon fresh grated ginger
2 teaspoons sea salt
1 cup brown sugar
1 cup plain yellow cornmeal
6 tablespoons butter
3 medium-sized sweet potatoes, baked, peeled, and mashed
5 large eggs, separated
2 teaspoons baking powder
2 tablespoons butter
½ cup pecans
½ cup pure maple syrup

Preheat oven to 350°F. Bring first four ingredients to a simmer in a 3-quart saucepan over medium heat. Whisk cornmeal into milk mixture in a slow, steady stream. Cook, whisking constantly, 2 to 3 minutes or until mixture thickens and pulls away from bottom of pan. Remove from heat and stir in butter. Cool 10 minutes.

Place potatoes in a large bowl; stir in cornmeal mixture. Stir in egg yolks and baking powder until well-blended.

Beat egg whites at high speed with an electric mixer until soft peaks form; fold into potato mixture. Spoon batter into a well-buttered 3-quart baking dish.

Melt 2 tablespoons butter and mix last 3 ingredients together, topping spoonbread with mixture prior to baking.

Bake at 350°F for 40 minutes or until golden brown and puffy. (Edges will be firm and center will still be slightly soft.) Cool 10 minutes on a wire rack before serving.

Berry Fool with Sweet Biscuits & Fresh Berries

Nate Allen

For Fool

6 cups red berries

½ cup sugar

Generous amount of heavy cream

For Biscuits

2 cups White Lily self-rising flour

⅓ cup butter, softened

Pinch salt

⅓ cup sugar

1½ cups buttermilk

Cook berries with sugar, purée, strain, and cool. Whip cream until stiff, and fold into berry mixture.

Work butter into dry ingredients until incorporated, then slowly add buttermilk. Turn onto floured surface and fold into thirds five times, always rolling down to 1-inch height. Cut into circles or squares and bake at 400°F for 10 minutes. Cut in half and top with fool. Add red berries. Place top of biscuit over berries.

"Food is the most powerful medicine we've got."
—DR. JOHN LaPUMA

Cathy Guthrie's Sorghum Caramels

Cathy Guthrie

Cathy Guthrie, owner of Doubletree Farm in Mars Hill, North Carolina, raises goats, makes molasses, chops wood, plows with draft horses, and holds it all together while fostering her children's musical inclinations, still making time to turn out handmade sorghum caramels.

2 cups sugar
2 cups (1 pint) sorghum syrup
1 cup butter
1 cup goat's milk (or cream)

Note: I use this caramel for making turtles, topping the caramel squares with chocolate.

Prepare a pan at least 8x8 inches with a greased or buttered tin foil liner.

Bring sugar, sorghum, and butter up to 224°F (this takes about 15–20 minutes). Add milk slowly and bring the temperature up to at least 245°F or "firm ball" stage on the candy thermometer. Again, this takes about 20 minutes.

Pour the hot mixture into prepared pan. Let it sit for at least 4 hours to cool down. Then turn out onto a cutting board and cut into strips and squares. Must be wrapped individually or they will stick together.

Sorghum Molasses Cookies

Makes 5 dozen

Polly Gott

My mother has always made the most succulent molasses cookies in the world. They are crisp on the outside, chewy on the inside, and they are great dipped in milk, especially when that milk comes straight from the cow, as it did all throughout my childhood. Experiment with baking times, depending on your oven. A longer cooking time makes them crisp through and through. A shorter cooking time leaves a bit of chewiness.

1½ cups shortening (butter is best)

2 cups sugar (1 white, 1 brown)

2 eggs

½ cup sorghum molasses (or Grandma's molasses if you can't find sorghum)

4 cups sifted flour

2 teaspoons baking soda

2 teaspoons cinnamon

2 teaspoons cloves

2 teaspoons ginger

Cream sugar and shortening. Beat in eggs, add sorghum and sifted dry ingredients. Roll into 1-inch balls and dip in granulated sugar. Place on baking sheet, 2 inches apart. Bake in moderate oven (375°F) for 15 minutes.

Black Cherry Clafoutis

SG Séguret

You can use any kind of cherries for this recipe, but the little black sweet cherries that were once prolific in old orchards throughout the South are the ones I always strive to find. If using a sour variety you may have to adjust the quantity of sugar. Traditionally, the pit is left in, and imparts (or so they say) a slight almond flavor to the dish. To make sure you really do detect the almond flavor, which goes delightfully with the cherries, I have added a small amount of almond extract here. Or if you have almond powder, you can use it in place of, or in combination with, the flour.

1¼ pounds black cherries
3 large eggs, at room
    temperature
½ cup all-purpose flour
1 teaspoon vanilla extract
⅛ teaspoon almond extract
½ cup sugar, plus extra for
    sprinkling
1⅓ cups whole milk
Butter for the baking dish

Preheat the oven to 375°F. Brush a shallow baking dish liberally with butter. Wash and stem the cherries. Lay them in a single layer in the baking dish. You may remove the pits in advance, or you may just leave them in. Don't forget to warn your guests if you choose to do the latter!

Mix the eggs, flour, vanilla and almond extracts, sugar, and milk together until smooth. Pour batter over the cherries and bake until the custard is just set (a knife poked in the center should emerge relatively clean), about 45 minutes. Sprinkle liberally with sugar, and serve warm or cold, but not too hot.

Cinnamon Bread Pudding
with Plum Compote and Bittersweet Chocolate Ganache

Peter Affatato

3 ripe plums (for compote)

½ lemon (for compote)

1 teaspoon granulated sugar (for compote)

½ cup 60% bittersweet chocolate chips (for ganache)

½ cup heavy cream (for ganache)

8-ounce loaf of your favorite egg bread (Challah is great), preferably a day or two old, cubed

For the Custard

1 cup whole milk

2 whole eggs

1 cup heavy cream

½ cup granulated sugar

2 egg yolks

½ teaspoon vanilla extract

Cinnamon to taste

Preheat oven to 325°F. Butter one (2½ quart) baking dish or little baking dishes 3 inches deep.

Combine milk and heavy cream in noncorrosive 1-quart pot. Place whole eggs, egg yolks, sugar, and vanilla in stainless mixing bowl, whisk until pale yellow, set aside. Heat milk and cream on stove top just until scalded. Remove milk and cream mixture from stove and slowly whisk into egg mixture.

Building

Put cubed bread into large mixing bowl, slowly pour half of egg and cream mixture over bread, and mix gently until your egg and cream mixture is absorbed into bread, trying not to break up bread cubes. In your baking dish, layer your soaked bread sprinkled with cinnamon at each level until you have come about a quarter inch from the rim of the dish. Slowly pour remaining egg and cream mixture into baking dish, pushing down on bread until soaked. Baking time will be about 45–60 minutes.

Baking

Take a large baking pan, big enough to hold your pudding dish, and set pudding in it. Place in oven and fill larger baking dish with hot tap water. Close oven and begin baking process. Bake until bread is toasted and dark golden and no custard pushes through when prodded with finger. Remove pudding from water bath and cool on rack for 30 minutes. It will be ready to serve at this point, or can be covered and refrigerated.

For the Plum Compote

While your pudding is baking, bring a 2½-quart pot half full of water to a boil, then reduce heat so water is at a simmer. Take plums and, with tip of knife, make slash ¼-inch deep on top side. Slowly put plums into pot of water for 30–45 seconds, remove from pot with slotted spoon into colander, and run under cold water for 30 seconds. Let cool for 10 minutes more. Gently peel skin from plums, split, remove pit, dice, toss with teaspoon of sugar, squeeze juice of ½ lemon, toss again, and set aside.

For the Ganache

Put your ½ cup heavy cream into small heavy-bottomed pot, on low heat, and bring temperature up slowly. Do not let boil. Put chocolate chips into heat-proof ceramic bowl large enough to accommodate your hot cream. Pour over, but do not stir. Let stand 5 minutes, then whisk gently until smooth and silky. Set aside.

To Serve

Remove pudding from baking dish, divide evenly, put on serving plates, and top with a tablespoon of Plum Compote. Drizzle with ganache and top with whipped cream.

"Food isn't just about sustenance in the physiological sense; it's about soul sustenance."

—IVY BRASHEAR

Blueberry Semifreddo

William Dissen

5 large eggs, yolks and whites
   separated
1 cup sugar, divided
3 ounces blueberry purée
2 tablespoons lime peel, finely
   zested
2 cups heavy cream

Line a 9x5x3-inch loaf pan with 2 layers of plastic wrap, leaving an overhang around all sides. Whisk together egg yolks, ½ cup sugar, blueberry purée, and lime zest in a medium metal bowl. Place bowl with yolks over a pot of simmering water and whisk constantly until the mixture thickens and an instant-read thermometer reads 160°F, about 3 minutes. Beat cream in another large bowl until peaks form. Reserve.

In another bowl, beat the egg whites until soft peaks form and gradually add ½ cup of sugar, 1 tablespoon at a time. Beat the sugar and egg white mixture until stiff but not dry. Fold the egg white mixture into the yolk mixture in 3 additions, followed by the whipped cream. Stir in until just incorporated. Spread the blueberry semifreddo mixture into the prepared loaf pan and fold the plastic wrap over the top to cover. Freeze overnight. To serve, take from freezer and remove plastic wrap. Using a sharp knife, cut the semifreddo into equal portions. Serve immediately.

Moonshine Donuts

Paul Rankin & Nick Nairn

1 cinnamon apple marble
   (or leftover pound) cake
250 grams (1⅔ cups) self-rising
   flour
Water to dilute
2 tablespoons moonshine
2 lemons, juiced
2 tablespoons caster (superfine)
   sugar (finer than granulated,
   but not as fine as powdered
   sugar)
Oil for deep-frying
Confectioner's sugar for dusting

For the Cherries

150 grams (⅔ cup) fresh
   cherries, pitted
200 grams (1 cup) dried sour
   cherries
100 milliliters (⅓ cup) red wine
Zest of 1 lemon
2 tablespoons moonshine
1 tablespoon caster sugar

For the Chocolate Sauce

250 grams (8 ounces) dark
   chocolate
200 milliliters (⅔ cup) double
   (heavy) cream

Remove the outer crusts of the cinnamon apple marble cake, and cut the cake into thick slices.

Make a batter by placing the flour in a large bowl and adding water until a medium-thick consistency is achieved.

Make a lemon syrup by mixing together the sugar, lemon juice, and moonshine. Next, pull the cake slices into chunks and dip into the lemon syrup, then into flour, and finally into the batter.

Deep fry at 180°C (356°F) until golden. Remove from the fryer and dust with confectioner's sugar.

For the Cherries

Mix together the dried sour cherries, red wine, and a little moonshine, and leave to soak. Next, in a hot pan, add the sugar and begin to caramelize. Add the fresh cherries and the moonshine, and ignite until the alcohol has burned off (or almost!).

Add the macerated sour cherry mixture to the pan and continue cooking until the sour cherries have softened. Add the lemon zest.

For the Chocolate Sauce

Place the chocolate and the cream in a large bowl over a bain-marie. Heat the cream slowly until the chocolate melts. Mix well and keep warm.

To Serve:

Place the donuts in the center of a plate. Add a scoop of ice cream (vanilla is ideal) and spoon over the warm chocolate sauce. Next, spoon over the cherries and add a splash of liquor.

Appendices

Southern Appalachian Heirloom Bean Terminology

Contributed by Bill Best

IT IS COMMON TO HEAR "old timers" speak of people who "don't know beans" about a particular subject. That means they know very little about what they are talking about. Since gardening is not a part of the lifestyle of many people today, we increasingly also have a problem of people "not knowing beans about beans." These definitions are put forth to inform people who don't know much about beans and to assist them in buying bean seeds for their gardens or purchasing fresh beans from growers or other sellers of beans. (It is a sign of the times that most of this information was common knowledge only 50 years ago.)

As heirloom beans continue to make a comeback in gardens, restaurants, and the marketplace, it will again be necessary to be able to identify them by type. An individual variety can be a combination of types. For example, a variety can be a long speckled greasy Cut-Short cornfield bean or a large multicolored bush butter bean.

Those who have never eaten heirloom beans are in for a treat, as more and more people are finding out, especially as the beans are becoming more available at farmers' markets and as more people are growing them in their gardens.

"In the unconscious mind, food equals love because food is our deepest and earliest connection with our caretaker."
—KATHRYN ZERBE, PSYCHIATRIST

Bush or Bunch Beans: There are very few heirloom bunch beans in the Southern Appalachians, but there are some quite good ones. Several are fall beans and have strings while a few are stringless. As a general rule, bush beans have tougher hulls than cornfield beans, which lessens their desirability. They also produce far fewer beans, which makes them less attractive to growers with limited space. Depending on variety, they can be broken and cooked when full or while pods are still tender, if they are varieties which become tough when full. Or, as with cornfield beans, they can be eaten as Shelly or dry beans as well. Most people feel that stringless beans have less flavor than ones that require stringing.

Butter Beans: Butter beans, very common in the deep South, are grown extensively in the Southern Appalachians as well. They are usually somewhat smaller than their cousin, the lima bean, but are very colorful. They must be shelled out for eating, either as Shelly beans or later as dry beans. Many families grow at least one variety of butter beans.

Cornfield Beans: Any climbing bean. Corn stalks traditionally served as the poles which beans used for climbing.

Crease Back Beans: A type of heirloom bean that has a crease in the outer portion of the bean hull. They are sometimes called creasy beans (not to be confused with greasy beans).

Cut-Short Beans: A type of bean where the seeds outgrow the hulls and lock the developing seeds against one another. This makes them appear square, rectangular, triangular, or even trapezoidal in form. Cut-Shorts are in high demand by traditional growers because of their high protein content. They are sometimes called bust-out beans because the dried hulls will often split apart vigorously after the bean pods have dried out and then become wet again by rain or even a heavy dew. This is nature's way of scattering seeds for the upcoming season.

Dry Beans: Any bean can be a dry bean since the term refers to the dry seeds of beans. Beans can be allowed to dry while in the hull or shelled out as Shelly beans and then allowed to dry while spread out on a flat surface. If the weather threatens, many gardeners will pick their beans while still in the Shelly stage rather than take a chance on the hulls becoming discolored, which might also discolor the seeds. Dry beans are typically rehydrated prior to cooking by soaking overnight or longer, sometimes pouring the water off several times before cooking them.

Fall or October Beans: These are beans which are typically planted later than other cornfield beans and which mature near the time the first frost appears. Typically, they have large seeds and sometimes have stringless hulls. They are often somewhat tougher than other heirloom beans which typically remain tender all the way to the Shelly stage and beyond. They can be eaten as green beans, as Shelly beans, or as dry beans. Many families plant at least one fall bean. There are also many varieties of bush fall beans.

Full Beans: This is a term used to describe a bean where the seed is fully mature within the hull and the bean is ready to harvest. Heirloom beans are traditionally harvested at the full stage whether they are to be used fresh, canned, pickled, or for making leather britches.

Greasy Beans: A name given to many heirloom bean varieties when the pods are slick and without the tight-knit fuzz of other beans. The slickness makes them appear to be greasy. Greasy beans are widely thought to be the highest-quality beans and are by far the highest priced, bringing in two to 10 times as much as other beans. Most greasy bean varieties are found in Western North Carolina and Eastern Kentucky but are spreading rapidly to other areas through farmers markets and heirloom seed outlets. Greasy Cut-Shorts are in very high demand.

Half-Runner Beans: This is a term given to many varieties of beans where the runner is roughly three to 10 feet long. It might be more accurate to say that there are quarter-runner beans, half-runner beans and full-runner beans, with full-runner beans climbing to 20 feet or more. Half-runners are very popular in the southern mountains, and this led to commercial seed companies starting to produce and sell seeds. This further led to the tough gene being implanted in most commercial half-runners and much unhappiness among traditional half-runner enthusiasts who want their beans to be both full and tender. At this time, many people are trying to locate and save the traditional half-runners which have never been "improved" by making them tough for mechanical harvest.

Leather Britches: Leather britches, also called shucky beans, shuck beans, and in some areas, fodder beans, are made from full green beans which have been strung, broken into pieces, and then dried. Traditionally, they are dried by running a needle and thread through each piece and hanging them up in long strings behind a wood cook stove to dry out as quickly as possible. They can also be dried by spreading them out in a greenhouse on bed sheets, newspapers, or window screens. Still another way of drying them is putting them on window screens on a tin roof and bringing them in at night, or even putting them in a junk car with windows rolled up on sunny days. Once eaten almost every day during winter and spring, they are now served mostly on special days such as family reunions, weddings, anniversaries, Thanksgiving, Christmas, New Year, and other holidays. Drying beans is the oldest way of preserving them and still very effective. Properly dried and cooked, they are delicious.

Pink Tip Beans: There are many varieties of pink tip beans. The term pink tip refers to the tip of the bean becoming pink in color as the bean becomes full. The tip becoming pink also indicates that the bean is ready to be picked for fresh eating, canning, or making leather britches. Seeds of pink tip varieties can be white, black, brown, tan, striped, mottled, or speckled, depending on variety.

Pole Beans: Same as cornfield beans. When some gardeners stopped growing corn in their gardens, poles often substituted for corn stalks. They are often used in teepee-style to give stability. More recently, poles have given way to trellises, which give more room and more sunshine to the bean vines. They can also be made stronger to survive better in windy weather.

Shelly Beans: This term refers to a bean shelled from a mature full bean before the hull and seed dry out. The beans are then cooked without the need for rehydration as would be the case with dry beans. Beans can also be frozen at the Shelly stage and cooked later as one would cook the freshly shelled beans. Shelly beans are very popular with many old-time gardeners and others who knew them as children.

Snap Beans: At one time most any bean picked green for eating fresh or drying would be called a snap bean since, after being strung, they would snap or break quickly and cleanly. With most commercial beans now having been bred to be tough and stringless to withstand mechanical harvesting without breaking, the term snap bean is rarely used since the modern bean doesn't snap or break cleanly. This is also why so many are now canned and cooked as whole beans before the seed begins to develop. However, most heirloom beans picked at the green stage, even when full, are still snap beans.

Soldier Beans: Having a crop of beans where the beans line up on the bean stem in formation, is a mark of having a good bean crop. When the beans are lined up one-by-one or two-by-two until the stem contains six to 12 beans, picking them is easy, and they can be gathered a handful at a time. Such beans are sometimes called soldier beans. The number of beans per stem is often limited by weather conditions, and too much heat will result in a lot of beans dropping off shortly after the bloom stage. At the same time, individual vines under good conditions may have 100 or more bean pods and 700–800 seeds.

String Beans: Most heirloom beans are string beans. This means they have at least one string per side while some have two on the inner section; one on each half, making three strings altogether but still easily removed. These strings have to be removed prior to cooking or drying. Exceptions to this rule are some varieties of October/fall beans. Many people, especially those who use beans as a principal part of their diet, won't plant or purchase beans that do not have strings since they consider them to be of poor quality, both in texture and in flavor.

Stringless Beans: Most beans produced by modern plant breeding, and most sold in commercial catalogues, are stringless beans. The downside of stringless is toughness. This is why commercial bean customers are advised to "Pick while young and tender" or "Don't let lumps (seeds) appear in your beans." Stringless beans typically have to be harvested before the protein (seed) appears.

Variants: Beans often mutate or cross and then grow back true to the new form. Variant is a word often used to characterize the new bean. Most such beans are then sold or distributed as a variant of the bean from which they mutated. However, within a few years, such beans usually assume their own names and have identities completely separate from the original parent bean. In the meantime, variants might even have their own variants. This is why there are so many heirloom bean varieties.

Wax Beans: A type of bean, usually yellow or light-colored in appearance, which has a hull somewhat thicker than other cornfield beans and which has a waxy feel to the touch. It is very often used in three-bean salads. This is a popular heirloom bean in some areas, not very well known in others, and virtually unknown in still other areas.

Additional Bean Terminology

Seed Shapes: Seed shapes can range from near perfectly round to oblong and nearly flat. Most are oval and elongated. Cut-Short varieties have varied shapes, with beans within a single hull being of many shapes because of the pressure of the seeds against one another within the hull during the growth period.

Seed Colors: Heirloom bean seeds come in many colors: They can be solid red, white, black, blue, purple, brown, tan, pink, beige, and other colors. They can be speckled with any number of colors of specks with contrasting background colors. They can be striped with the stripes being of many colors and also have many background colors, such as black on white or dark brown on tan. And they can be mottled, which is when there is a combination of specks, stripes, and smudges. Some are solid in color except for the eyes, which are of a different color. Others are mostly of one color with smudges of another color in random patterns, all within the same hull. One bean with striking colors is the Turkey Craw bean, which is tan on one end, buff on the other, and speckled in between. Some people are so enthusiastic about colored beans that they use them to create jewelry.

"Corn, beans, and squash—the 'three sisters'—grow together because of their symbiotic relationship. Corn removes nitrogen from the soil, and beans replace it. Cornstalks provide a natural trellis for the bean plants to climb on. Low-growing squash plants create shade and hold in moisture."
—FRED SAUCEMAN

Examples of Heirloom Bean Varieties

Agate

Amish Nuttle

Anellino Yellow

Annie Jackson

Annie's Tasty Green
   Pod

Appaloosa

Aquadulce

Arikara Yellow

Arlie Grizzle Cornfield

Aztec Red Kidney

Beurre de
   Rocquencourt

Black Coat

Black Russian

Black Valentine

Blue Coco

Blue Jay

Blue Top Bottle Greasy
   Cut-Short

Broad Windsor

Brown Caseknife

Calypso

Cameleon

Canadian Wild Goose

Canadian Wonder

Carr

Cherokee Trail of Tears

Clova Collins Cornfield

Coco Jaune de Chine

Coco Sophie

Colony String

Comtesse de Chambord

Crimson Flowered

Deseronto Potato Bean

Dolloff

Dragon's Tongue

Duane Baptiste Potato

Early Mohawk

Early Riser

Early Yellow Six Weeks

Empress

Envy

Fisher

Flagg

Fortin's Family

Frijol en Seco Pinto

Ga Ga Hut Pinto

Good Mother Stallard

Grandma Nellie's
   Mushroom

Great Northern

Hanna Hank

Harder Heirloom

Henderson's Bush

Heritage Dore

Hickler Stick

Hidatsa

Hidatsa Red

Hidatsa Shield Figure

Hopi Black

Improved Golden Wax

Iroquois Cornbread

Jacob's Cattle

Jesse Fisk

Jessy's Family
   Heirloom

John's

Jumbo Roma

Kentucky Wonder Bush

Kentucky Wonder Pole

Lazy Wife

Lena's Bean

Lena Spraybash's

Light Brown Zebra

Limelight

Little White Rice

Littlefield's Special

Logan County Greasy
   Cut-Short

Low's Champion

Maccarone

Mandan Black

Martoc

Marvel of Venice

Mary Ison's Little
   Brown Bunch

Mayflower

Mennonite K Triple A

Mennonite Purple
   Stripe

Minnesota 1940's

Molasses Face

Montcalm

Mrs. Marotti's Romano

Nebraska Beauty

O'Driscoll
Orca
Painted Lady
Painted Pony
Peck to a Hill
Pepa de Zapallo
Peregion
Pete Ingram Fall Bean
Pfaelzer Juni
Pink Tip Fall Bean
Piros Feher
Pisarecka Zlutoluske
Polish Pea Bean
Polish Pole
Provider
Purple Peacock (Beige Seeded)
Rattlesnake Snap
Red Peanut
Red Swan
Red Valentine
Refugee

Rogers Family Greasy Cut-Short
Roja de Seda
Romano 14
Round White Baking
Royalty Purple Pod
Sadie's Horse Bean
Sandy Mush Greasy
Scarlet Beauty
Scarlet Runner
Snowcap
Soldat de la Beauce
Southern Soldier
Speckled Algonquin
Steeves Caseknife
Stoltfus String
Stringless Green Pod
Sultan's Green Crescent
Sultan's Golden Crescent
Superlative

Swedish Brown
Sweeney Family Heirloom
Tar Heel
Tendergreen
Tene's Beans
Thibodeau de Comte Beauce
Tiger's Eye
Triomphe de Farcy
True Cranberry
Tung's
Turkey Craw
Ukrainian Comrades
Vanderpol Six Weeks
Vermont Cranberry
White Caseknife
Worcester Indian
Wren's Egg Fall Bean (tender hull)
Wren's Egg Fall Bean (tough hull)

Ramps

Contributed by Denny Trantham

THE RAMP, SOMETIMES CALLED WILD leek, is a wild onion native to North America. Though the bulb resembles that of a scallion, the beautiful flat, broad leaves set it apart. According to John Mariani, author of *The Encyclopedia of American Food and Drink,* the word "ramp" comes from "rams," or "ramson," an Elizabethan dialect rendering of the wild garlic.

Ramps grow from South Carolina to Canada, and in many areas they're considered a spring delicacy and even a reason for celebration. West Virginia is well known for its many festivals and events in celebration of the ramp, as is North Carolina and Tennessee. The flavor and odor of ramps is usually compared to a combination of onions and garlic, and the garlic odor is particularly strong. Strong enough, in fact, that even ramp-lovers will advise caution. If you sit down to a big meal of ramps, don't be surprised if people continue to keep their distance after a few days have passed!

Caution aside, ramps add a wonderful and uniquely pungent flavor to soups, egg dishes, casseroles, rice dishes, and potato dishes. Use them raw or cooked in any recipe calling for scallions or leeks, or cook them in a more traditional way, scrambled with eggs or fried with potatoes. Since ramps aren't cultivated in the way leeks are, they're much easier to clean. Just cut off roots, rinse thoroughly, and scrub off any excess dirt on the bulbs.

Ramps aren't available for long, but you can chop and freeze them for cooked dishes. The green tops are milder in flavor and are usually used along with the bulbs. I chop about half of the green leaves separately, air-dry them for a few hours, then freeze them in an air-tight container for future use as a seasoning.

Author's Note: If harvesting ramps yourself, make sure you leave a large portion of the patch behind so that it will continue to proliferate. Ideally, you should have a knife in hand to trim and re-plant the roots as you go. If you buy the ramps with the roots on and have a backwoods area, try tucking the bottom cuttings under the forest foliage and be sure to check your spot next spring.

Cutting-Edge Appalachian Chefs, Growers, Butchers, and Neighbors

So many innovators abound in this region of riches, this list is but a beginning. Make your own list of those who inspire you, who have shared with you the wealth of their table. The circle is ever widening.

Adam Hayes (NC)

Allan Benton (TN)

Anne Arbaugh (WV)

Anne Hart (WV)

Annie Pettry (KY)

Anthony Lamas (KY)

Ashley Christensen (NC)

Ashley English (NC)

Barbara Kingsolver (VA)

Barbara Swell (NC)

Bill Best (KY)

Bill Collier (PA)

Bill Justice (OH)

Billy Allin (GA)

Bradley Griffin (VA)

Britt Saylor (VA)

Cassidy Dabney (TN)

Carla Hall (TN)

Cathy Guthrie (NC)

Chris Hastings (AL)

Chris Newsome (AL)

Chris Weihs (NC)

Dale Hawkins (WV)

Damian Heath (WV)

Daniel Lindley (TN)

Debby Maugans (NC)

Denny Trantham (NC)

Edward Lee (KY)

Edwin Bloodworth (NC)

Elliott Moss (NC)

Frank Stitt (AL)

Fred Sauceman (TN)

George McMillan (AL)

Gunnar Thompson (VA)

Hari Pulapaka (FL)

Harper Bradshaw (VA)

Ian Boden (VA)

Jacob Sessoms (NC)

James Boyce (AL)

Jamie Ager (NC)

Jason Roy (NC)

Jassen Campbell (VA)

Jay Zuspan (MD)

Joe Scully (NY, NC)

John Currence (MS)

John Fleer (TN, NC)

Joseph Lenn (TN)

Josh Feathers (TN)

Kathy Cary (KY)

Katie Hoffman (TN)

Katie Bennett (TN)

Kevin Gillespie (GA)

Kyle Krieger (VA)

Kyle McKnight (NC)

Levon Wallace (TN)

Liz Miller (TN)

Marion Ohlinger (WV)

Mark Rosenstein (NC)

Marty Lewis (NC)

Mary Collins-Shepard (TN)

Michael Hudman (TN)

Mike Ferrari (NC)

Mike Moore (NC)

Nate Allen (NC)

Nathalie Dupree (GA, SC)

Peter Affatato (NC)

Peter & Polly Gott (NC)

Ralph Lewis (NC)

Richard Arbaugh (WV)

Richard & Holly Giles (NY)

Ronni Lundy (KY, NC)

Ryan Campbell (ME)

Ryan Smith (GA)

Sarah Steffan (TN)

Sean Brock (SC, TN)

Shelley Cooper (TN)

Sheri Castle (NC)

Stephen & Dawn Robertson (NC)

Steven Goff (NC)

Tandy Wilson (TN)

Tom Michaels (TN)

Travis Milton (VA)

Tyler Brown (TN)

Vicki Blizzard (TN)

Vivian Howard (NC)

William Dissen (NC)

Resources

Farms, Consultants, Products, Organizations, Educational Opportunities

Appalachian Highlands Consulting offers speaking and consulting by Dr. Jean Haskell, co-editor of the *Encyclopedia of Appalachia* and former director of ETSU's Center for Appalachian Studies and Services. jeanhaskell415@gmail.com

Appalachian Regional Commission (ARC), based in Washington, D.C., is a federal-state partnership that works for sustainable community and economic development in Appalachia. www.arc.gov

Appalachian South Folklife Center, based in Pipestem, West Virginia, is dedicated to the celebration of mountain heritage, freedom, and self-reliance, and presents programs and services that reflect a pride in being mountaineers. www.folklifecenter.org

Appalachian Sustainable Agriculture Project (ASAP), based in Asheville, North Carolina, helps local farms thrive, links farmers to markets and supporters, and builds healthy communities through connections to local food. www.asapconnections.org

Appalworks, based in Gray, Tennessee, offers a range of customized services focusing on aspects of Appalachian culture, history, and heritage. www.appalworks.com

Benton's Country Hams, based in North Madisonville, Tennessee, has honed the dry-curing of hams and bacon into a culinary art, and has catapulted the products from a simple breakfast mainstay into the world of gourmet cooking. Products can be shipped anywhere in the United States. www.bentonscountryhams2.com

Buck Hill Farm, a family-operated Sugar House in Jefferson, NY, in the heart of the Catskill Mountains, turns out maple syrup for the finest restaurants in New York as well as neighboring farmers' markets. Serving Sunday breakfasts and offering maple products through their store, they nourish the community surrounding them with exceptional sweetness. www.buckhillfarm.com

Carolina Bison began in 1985 as King's Farm, a multigenerational, family-run farm that raised bison in western Pennsylvania. When Dr. King moved to Asheville, purchasing farmland in Leicester, the venture became Carolina Bison Farm. Bison is a nutrient-dense meat that is low-fat and low in cholesterol with high levels of vitamin E, omega-3 essential fatty acids, and protein. Native to this continent, bison were called "good medicine" by Native Americans, who relied on bison for survival. www.drkings.com

Carolina Farm Stewardship Association (CFSA), based in North Carolina, helps people in the Carolinas grow and eat local, organic food by advocating for fair farm and food policies, building the systems that organic family farms need to thrive, and educating communities about local, organic farming. www.carolinafarmstewards.org

Center for Appalachian Studies & Services (CASS), located in Johnson City at East Tennessee State University, documents and showcases Appalachia's past, celebrates its cultural heritage, and promotes an understanding of the influences that shape its identity. www.etsu.edu/cas/cass

Foxfire, the legacy, was founded in 1966 in Rabun Gap, Georgia, as a means of making English engaging to students who would rather have been hunting, fishing, or anything but sitting in a classroom. Beginning as a magazine, with stories collected and written by the students themselves, it progressed to a series of books, a museum and heritage center, and ultimately an approach to teaching and learning that has inspired many educators since its beginning. Currently operated by an extensive board of directors, Foxfire is, in this year of 2016, celebrating 50 years of community-based education.

Harvest Table Restaurant, in Meadowview, Virginia, began as an extension of the bestselling book *Animal, Vegetable, Miracle*, written by Director Steven Hopp, his wife—Barbara Kingsolver—and two daughters. The story about one family's yearlong experiment to eat in-season locally grown foods has become far more than just their story. www.harvesttablerestaurant.com

Highlander Research and Education Center, based in Newmarket, Tennessee, is a place where leaders, networks, and movement strands come together to advance a multi-racial, inter-generational movement for social and economic justice in the Appalachian region. www.highlandercenter.org

International Association of Culinary Professionals (IACP) is a multifaceted membership, which includes chefs, restaurateurs, foodservice operators, writers, photographers, stylists, marketers, nutritionists, and academia, hailing from hospitality, tourism, publishing, and many other disciplines. www.iacp.com

J.Q. Dickinson Salt-Works is operated by seventh-generation salt-makers brother and sister Nancy Bruns and Lewis Payne. The history of Appalachian salt is deeply personal to their family, whose Dickinson ancestors first drilled for brine in 1817 using a hollowed-out tree trunk for piping, and established the family farm along the Kanawha River. www.jqdsalt.com

Seasonal School of Culinary Arts (SSCA), based in Asheville, North, Carolina, with additional sessions in Ithaca, Sonoma, and Paris, inspires home chefs and culinary professionals alike to gather food consciously, treat it with skill and respect, and share it with passion, furthering the notion that the most important moments we spend are those partaken with friends and family around the table. www.schoolofculinaryarts.org

Southern Foodways Alliance (SFA). The Southern Foodways Alliance documents, studies, and explores the diverse food cultures of the changing American South. It is a member-supported organization based at the University of Mississippi's Center for the Study of Southern Culture. www.southernfoodways.org

Southern Appalachian Archives-Mars Hill University. The Southern Appalachian Archives is a rich storehouse of manuscripts and collections which document regional and local history. www.mhu.edu/ramsey-center/southern-appalachian-archives

Spinning Spider Creamery is an artisan goat dairy nestled in a mountain cove on Bailey Mountain in Madison County, North Carolina. www.spinningspidercreamery.com

Steve Tweed is a self-taught photographer from Madison County, North Carolina specializing in Appalachian culture, architecture, and people, with a passion for all three. He and his wife, Lou Anne, live in the Shelton Laurel Community, where Steve has spent the majority of his life. Riding back roads, studying local history and folklore, and just shooting the breeze are among his favorite hobbies.

Sustainable Mountain Agriculture Center, in Berea, Kentucky, operated by Bill Best, is dedicated to saving and propagating heirloom seeds. www.heirlooms.org

Table on Ten is a gathering place in the town of Bloomville, New York, in the Western Catskills, and a hub for the farmers and artists who populate the area of Delaware County, just west of the Hudson Valley. The food does double duty both as nourishment and as an advertisement for the local farms, many of which maintain small stands for the public. www.tableonten.com

Tater Gap Garlic, organically grown in Madison County, North Carolina, offers both seed and culinary samples of multiple varieties acclimated to a mountain climate. www.tatergapgarlic.com

Three Graces Dairy (Ferguson Farm) is a historic farm in the Shelton Laurel area of Western North Carolina. The dairy is a small-scale multitasking environment employing local people who share their knowledge of the community and their wisdom in all things land and animal. www.threegracesdairy.com

Turtle Island Preserve, brainchild of Eustace Conway, celebrates lifestyle practices of an earlier people, including cultivation of the soil, tool skills, foraging experiences, and survival techniques. An eye-opener to a new generation, it is a reminder of how life has been lived in Appalachia throughout the ages. www.turtleislandpreserve.org

Waddell Media is an award-winning producer of lifestyle formats, high-quality documentaries, and factual programs for the UK, Irish, and international markets. www.waddellmedia.com

"Food to a large extent is what holds a society together, and eating is closely linked to deep spiritual experiences."
—PETER FARB AND GEORGE ARMELAGOS, *CONSUMING PASSIONS: THE ANTHROPOLOGY OF EATING*

Contributing Chefs

Peter Affatato, creator of longtime flagship Nona Mia in West Asheville, also helped develop Savoy and his previous restaurant known as 28806. His passion is the Italian-American cuisine of grandmothers.

Nate Allen, winner of *Cooking Light's* Small-Town Chef Award, 2011 WNC Best Chef, a graduate of Johnson & Wales in Providence, and nominee for the Rising Star Chef Award from *Food & Wine Magazine*, operates the innovative Spoon Bar in addition to his flagship Knife & Fork in Spruce Pine, North Carolina. www.knifeandforknc.com

Bill Best is a Kentucky seed saver, originally from Haywood County, North Carolina. Author of *Saving Seeds, Preserving Taste: Heirloom Seed Savers in Appalachia*, as well as numerous articles on the subject of seeds, he is rewriting the story of Jack and the Beanstalk, with Jack poised to win against the giant ConAgra. "I work with tomatoes for money," he says, "and beans for love." An heirloom is a seed that will reproduce itself. It's not a hybrid. An heirloom will breed true, whereas hybrids produce something different the following year. The seeds are usually passed on from generation to generation, as a piece of jewelry or fine furniture, hence the term heirloom. www.heirlooms.org

Vicki Blizzard, co-author of the *Jessiehouse, Georgia* cookbook, served as helpmeet to Dr. Tom Michaels when the first *Tuber melanosporum* were found in his orchard and he was perplexed as to how to market them immediately, before spoilage set in. Her connection to the Knoxville, Tennessee, food scene led to the eventual collaboration of Dr. Michaels with the crew at Blackberry Farm, and the inclusion of an orchard at that iconic resort. The recipe included here, laced with truffles, was inspired by her family.

Edwin Bloodworth began his culinary career at the age of 14 working at a family-style restaurant in Sparta, North Carolina. The owner was a tough and intimidating old man and the chef was a small, chain-smoking, foul-mouthed French woman. Edwin's next job was in the kitchen of Roaring Gap Club, working beside Greenbrier graduates, then at The Gamekeeper in Boone, North Carolina, as part of the opening team. This was followed by the Resort at Squaw Creek under Chef Jacques Cornelis and Michael Plapp, then Four Square in Durham, North Carolina; the Town House in Chilhowie, Virginia; Seven Sows & Bourbon, Lex 18, and Nightbell in Asheville; and most recently The Cliffs at Walnut Cove. His focus is on supporting local farmers and artisans, and exploring the wild foods the region has to offer, in an attempt to offer a "New Appalachian Cuisine." www.rootsculinary.blogspot.com

James Boyce's motto, for his numerous Huntsville, Alabama, restaurants is "Eat Simply. Eat Smart. Eat Well." The 20-year industry veteran launched his culinary career at New York's venerable Le Cirque, where he worked for six years under the tutelage of Daniel Boulud. While working in New York, Boyce studied at the Culinary Institute of America (CIA) in Hyde Park, graduating with top honors. In 1990, Boyce made his first trip west to The Phoenician,

where he worked with former chef de cuisine, Alex Stratta. After an initial five years with The Phoenician, he went to Caesar's Palace in Las Vegas as chef de cuisine at Palace Court. He joined Loews Coronado Bay Resort as executive chef in 1995. After earning a second Mobil Five-Star award for Studio, he relocated his family to Huntsville to begin new culinary endeavors with the development of his own company, Boyce Restaurant Concepts. Each restaurant within the Boyce Restaurant Concepts portfolio offers guests unique tastes and experiences which combine to make Downtown Historic Huntsville a compelling travel and dining destination. www.chefjamesboyce.com

Mary Collins-Shepard is a Techniques Class instructor for Williams-Sonoma in Knoxville, Tennessee, where she enjoys not only creating and sharing fresh, healthy dishes but teaching others to do so as well, feeding both of her passions simultaneously. She has, for years, created magic behind the scenes at the Seasonal School of Culinary Arts, and was a contributor to the recent recipe collection *Farmer & Chef Asheville*.

William Dissen, current owner of The Market Place Restaurant in Asheville, hails from West Virginia, where he grew up watching his grandmother cook straight from the garden. Chef Dissen has received the accolade of Rising Star Chef, and was named one of "40 Chefs Under 40" by Mother Nature Network. The Monterey Bay Aquarium gave him the title of Seafood Watch Ambassador, appointing him to their Blue Ribbon Task Force. With a degree from the CIA, he worked as chef at the Greenbriar Resort in West Virginia, and then in Charleston, South Carolina, and most recently picked up the reins of The Market Place Restaurant, where he has been named one of America's "Most Sustainable Chefs" and ever strives to create innovative farm-to-table cuisine utilizing ingredients and artisan products from within 100 miles of the restaurant. www.marketplace-restaurant.com

Nathalie Dupree, the first woman since Julia Child to film more than 100 cooking shows for public television (300 is her count), and author of 14 cookbooks including *Mastering the Art of Southern Cooking,* has helped bring Southern cooking to the nation's attention. Recognizing the contributions of European and African cooks, she emphasizes traditional ingredients and foodways that

can be traced back through the Great Depression of the 1930s to the Civil War. Based for years in Atlanta, where she helped citizens of the state to preserve and expand their culinary heritage, she now resides and works out of Charleston, South Carolina. www.nathalie.com

Ashley English, author of seven books including *Keeping Chickens*, *Quench* and *Homemade Gatherings*, lives in Candler, North Carolina, with her husband and young son, where she strives constantly to live what she writes. www.smallmeasure.com

John Fleer, chef owner of Rhubarb in Asheville, and former long-time Executive Chef at Blackberry Farm as well as Canyon Kitchen in Cashiers, brings both elegance and eloquence to the table. www.rhubarbasheville.com

Polly Gott and her husband, **Peter Gott**, in addition to being my beloved parents, were homesteaders in the 1960s, before the back-to-the-land movement became recognized as such. They made a life of growing everything they eat, as simply as possible. Their 218-acre farm in Madison County, North Carolina, has long been a mecca for aspiring homesteaders, artists, and musicians from all over the country and from all over the world.

Bradley Griffin is sous chef at The Harvest Table Restaurant in Meadowview, Virginia. Originally from High Point, North Carolina, Bradley worked at the Omni Grove Park Inn in Asheville, and the Green Park Inn and Blowing Rock Alehouse before becoming part of the Harvest Table community. He lives in Abingdon, Virginia. www.harvesttablerestaurant.com

Cathy Guthrie, owner of Doubletree Farm in Mars Hill, North Carolina, raises goats, makes molasses, chops wood, plows with draft horses, and holds it all together while fostering her children's musical inclinations, still making time to turn out handmade sorghum caramels.

Anne Hart has opened 12 restaurants in fine dining and casual themes in Atlanta, Rochester, Boston, and Washington, D.C., prior to opening Provence Market Café in Bridgeport, West Virginia, in May 2002. Hart was included in the inaugural edition of Best Chefs America, as well as Best Chefs of the South, in 2013. www.provencemarketcafe.com

Katie Hoffman is the founder and owner of Appalworks, a company that provides custom-designed programs, events, publications, and performances that promote Appalachian cultural heritage and artistry. A performer of traditional ballads, singer-songwriter, and scholar specializing in Appalachian Studies, Katie has worked with Dr. Jean Haskell, on a local food initiative for the Appalachian Regional Commission that focused on Appalachian food as sustainable, place-based economic development. Katie and her husband, Brett Tiller, raise a big garden and strive to eat as seasonally and locally as possible. Brett's mother has a treasure trove of traditional recipes, collected over the years from church, community, and family, and Katie scours them to find the most traditional recipes in the boxes and notebooks of handwritten material. As she cooks, she is often assisted by her stepdaughter Maria Tiller, who helps dice, chop, and bake as she participates in preserving her family's culinary heritage. Katie and Maria collaborated on choosing, testing, and writing the recipes included in this volume. www.appalworks.com

Imogene Lewis, mother of four active children, didn't actually cook very often. Her husband, Ralph, a bluegrass musician, was often on the road, and when he returned, he was the one who enjoyed messing around in the kitchen. But her few standbys, one of which is featured here, are ever dear to her children's hearts.

Marty Lewis is a gifted and prolific songwriter whose music has been recorded by Sons of Ralph, Open Road, Norfolk Southern Lawmen, 40 West, and The Lids. As a child, Marty and his brother Don toured with their father and Bill Monroe during school breaks as the youngest Bluegrass Boys, including an appearance at the Grand Ole Opry. He has performed on occasion with Chubby Wise and Kenny Baker, Vassar Clements, and Hank Thompson, and has recorded with numerous other groups. On stage, he often showcases songs of his beloved Madison County, followed by virtuoso renditions of Southern rock classics. Equally at home in the kitchen and in the woods, Marty delights in hunting deer and reeling in trout, and coming home with a bagful of ramps which he then turns into a huge dish to be shared with his extensive family. www.sonsofralph.com

Ralph Lewis is the seventh son born of another seventh son, a symbol of a lucky man in the mountains. He picked up mandolin and guitar at an early age, appearing with his siblings as The Lewis Brothers, and later with The Carolina Pals and The Piney Mountain Boys. In the 1970s, he joined Bill Monroe and the Bluegrass Boys and toured Europe, Japan, and the United States, and appeared regularly on the Grand Ole Opry. In more recent decades he and his sons Marty and Don have been Asheville mainstays, performing widely as The Sons of Ralph. Adept at both the high lonesome sound of bluegrass and the rhythms of rock and roll, as well as the haunting melodies of country, Ralph's music sounds as if it were carved out of the mountains themselves. His recipes, which have kept a family of six close to his side even through all the years of touring, are still coveted by his children today. www.sonsofralph.com

Debby Maugans, author of *Small-Batch Baking*, *Small-Batch Baking for Chocolate Lovers*, and co-author of *Farmer & Chef Asheville,* also developed the recipes for Fannie Flagg's best-selling *Whistle Stop Café Cookbook*. For seven years she wrote a popular weekly food column for Alabama's largest circulated newspaper, *The Birmingham News*. She currently writes and styles food for print, web, and video production, including recipe development for The Old Mill in Pigeon Forge. www.small-batchbaking.com

Tom Michaels holds a doctorate in plant pathology from Oregon State University. In 2000, he planted his first truffle orchard in East Tennessee (Tennessee Truffle), capturing the attention of *New York Times* food writer Molly O'Neill. He has supplied restaurants such as Blackberry Farm, as well as other restaurants from New York to Atlanta, and is recognized by chefs such as Thomas Keller and Daniel Boulud as the prime States-side source for the elusive *Tuber melanosporum*. www.tennesseetruffle.com

Nick Nairn is a Scottish chef who runs two cooking schools, one in Aberdeen and the other in Port of Menteith, Scotland. In 1986, he opened his first restaurant, Braeval, through which he won his first Michelin Star, and in 1997, he opened Nairn's restaurant in Glasgow. By this time he'd also begun his successful television career with appearances on the BBC's "Ready Steady Cook," and his own series, "Wild Harvest," "Wild Harvest 2," and "Island Harvest." Further shows included "Nick Nairn and the Dinner Ladies," and a winning appearance on "Great British Menu," which resulted in his cooking lunch for The Queen on her 80th birthday. Nick also runs Nick Nairn Consulting with two Hilton partnership restaurants, Native in Aberdeen and The Kailyard in

Dunblane. He works with high-caliber businesses where food is an integral part. He is author of 11 books and a regular contributor to food publications. www.nicknairncookschool.com

Paul Rankin is a celebrity chef from Ballywalter, County Down, Northern Ireland. In 1989, Paul Rankin opened Roscoff, the restaurant that was to become the first to win a Michelin Star in Northern Ireland. Soon after opening, it became the favorite meeting place for the Belfast business and arts community, and people traveled from Dublin simply to experience what was considered to be the best cooking in Northern Ireland at the time. His first foray into television was in the series "Gourmet Ireland," produced by Irish company Waddell Productions, and shown on both BBC and RTE. He has since been a regular chef on the BBC cookery program "Ready Steady Cook." In 1999, Rankin was the first chef from Northern Ireland to be awarded a Michelin Star. www.rankinselection.com

Mark Rosenstein, creator of Asheville, North Carolina's first fine dining and farm-to-table restaurant The Market Place, before farm-to-table was even a byword, has recently turned from life behind a hot stove to celebrating the finer things of life, while continuing to orchestrate new restaurant start-ups and culinary endeavors in the greater Asheville area. His book *In Praise of Apples* is a fine tribute to that versatile ingredient. His newest venture, built entirely out of recycled shipping containers, is called Smoky Park Supper Club. www.smokypark.com

Jason Roy, chef owner of Asheville's beloved Biscuit Head, formerly of LAB (Lexington Avenue Brewery), is an innovative powerhouse who welcomes all with his infectious smile as he does things with biscuits that no one else would dare think about! www.biscuitheads.com

Fred Sauceman, a member of the Southern Foodways Alliance, is the editor of that organization's *Cornbread Nation 5: The Best of Southern Food Writing*, published by the University of Georgia Press in 2010, in partnership with the University of Mississippi. He is creator of the book *Home and Away: A University Brings Food to the Table*, published by ETSU in 2000, and author of a three-volume book series, *The Place Setting: Timeless Tastes of the Mountain South, from Bright Hope to Frog Level*, about the foodways of Appalachia. As a cousin of the Sauceman Brothers, early country music recording artists, he recognizes the powerful link between music and food.

Joe Scully's first restaurant job in 1977 was as a host at a very busy Houlihan's Old Place in Hackensack, New Jersey. In 1987, he entered the Culinary Institute of America in Hyde Park, New York, where he graduated first in his class. He accepted a position at the Waldorf-Astoria hotel, and a year later was given a fellowship at The Culinary Institute's Escoffier Room restaurant. Shortly thereafter, he became the executive sous chef at the Cherokee Town and Country Club in Atlanta, where he won numerous culinary competition awards and co-founded two distinct food-manufacturing companies. In subsequent years, Joe held executive chef positions at Indigo Coastal Grill and The Druid Hills Golf Club in Atlanta, as well as at the United Nations in New York City, prior to making Asheville his home. Currently, Joe is chef/owner of three of Asheville's most distinctive and popular food operations: Corner Kitchen, Chestnut and Corner Kitchen Catering. www.chestnutasheville.com

Denny Trantham served for many years as executive chef at Asheville's Grove Park Inn Resort & Spa, and is now the spokesperson for Southern Foods. He holds, among many other accolades, the title of Best Chef of the Year (2013) from the North Carolina American Culinary Foundation. www.twitter.com/denny_trantham

"Appalachian ingredients and practices change over the decades, but creativity still pushes and pulls us along. Like our summer gardens, our food culture needs creative preservation if we expect it to last. How do we preserve not only our half runner beans, but our recipes, stories, folklore, and all of our kitchen arts in forms that serve us well in this moment and will also last? Creativity isn't a luxury; it keeps us alive."

—SHERI CASTLE

Recipe Index

"To create a dish, one starts with an idea and a number of ingredients… The goal is not to punctiliously follow instructions on a printed page; the goal is to duplicate a taste."
— JACQUES PEPIN

About the Author

Susi Gott Séguret, Certified Culinary Professional and Certified Specialist of Wine, hails from the depths of Appalachia in Madison County, North Carolina, but honed her culinary skills in France, where she resided for over 20 years, earning a diploma in Gastronomy and Taste from the Cordon Bleu and the *Université de Reims* while restoring a centuries-old stone barn, raising a family, and presenting Appalachian music to a European audience.

Editor of a dozen cookbooks and contributor to several compilations, Susi serves as personal chef and culinary journalist, and directs the Seasonal School of Culinary Arts with sessions in four corners of the globe: Asheville, Ithaca, Sonoma and Paris. She also orchestrates a series of ultra-elegant wine dinners known as the Asheville Wine Experience, and the gustatory extravaganza, the Asheville Truffle Experience.

Passionate about elements of taste and style, and how they extend from our palate into our daily lives, Susi strives to blend food, music, words, and images into a tapestry for the senses, which she shares generously with all who cross her path.

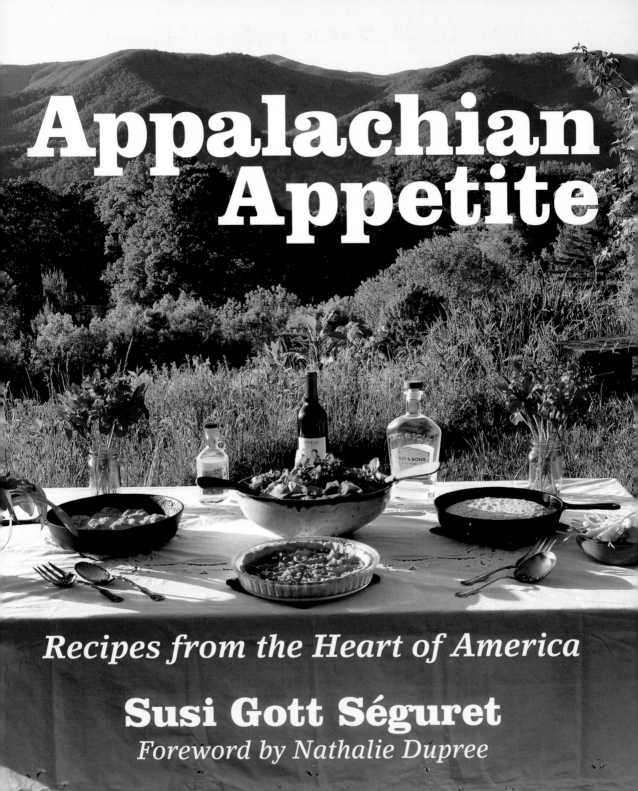

Appalachian Appetite

Appetite

Recipes from the Heart of America

Susi Gott Séguret

Foreword by Nathalie Dupree

Appalachian Appetite

Text copyright © 2016 SG Séguret

Library of Congress Cataloging-in-Publication Data is available upon request.
ISBN: 978-1-57826-657-9

COVER AND INTERIOR DESIGN BY CAROLYN KASPER
ALL PHOTOS ©SG SÉGURET, EXCEPT PAGES XVI, XVII,
15, 20–21, 28, 119, 203, 226, 232, AND 236-237
©STEVE TWEED; PAGE 49 ©MARK ROSENSTEIN; PAGE 75 ©PETER GOTT;
PAGE 92 ©CAROLINE WAY; AND PAGE 112 (LEFT) © BRADLEY GRIFFIN

Printed in the United States
10 9 8 7 6 5 4 3 2 1

"The act of cooking is the bridge between nature and culture."
—MICHAEL POLLAN

JAN 2 5 2017